Praise

"Melanie Faith has crafted everything you need to write a nonfiction book that is sought after by readers and that successfully sells. She stays with the writer before, during, and after the writing process. Using her tips and tricks for success, you'll have everything you need for your book to be successful and relevant for years to come, no matter what the subject."
ANTONIA ALBANY, AUTHOR OF *IN THIS MOMENT: MAKING THE MOST OF YOUR SENIOR YEARS*

"Melanie Faith's latest writing guidebook is everything and I mean everything (from pre-writing to post-publication) a writer needs to know about crafting a successful nonfiction reference book. The format enables the reader to use it in whatever way it works for them. Instructional and inspirational."
MARI L. MCCARTHY, AWARD-WINNING AUTHOR OF *JOURNALING POWER, HEAL YOUR SELF WITH JOURNALING POWER*

"Melanie Faith gives aspiring reference book writers far more than just a detailed road map from inspiration to publication. Her enthusiasm, support and expertise read like a chat with a wise friend. By the end you'll be ready to grab your paper, pens, laptop, or tablet and start writing."
LEE ANN SMITH, REFERENCE ASSISTANT

About the Author

Melanie Faith likes to wear many professional hats, including as a poet, photographer, prose writer, professor, editor, and tutor. Imagination and possibility are her favorite sidekicks. She especially enjoys writing nonfiction craft books that assist fellow authors on their writing paths.

Learn more about her writing process, writing classes, and latest projects at:
www.melaniedfaith.com

WRITING it REAL

Crafting a Reference Book that Sells

Melanie Faith, MFA

A catalogue record for this
book is available from the
NATIONAL
LIBRARY   National Library of Australia
OF AUSTRALIA

Other Books by this Author

Writing it Real: Creating an Online Course
for Fun and Profit

In a Flash!: Writing & Publishing Dynamic Flash Prose

Poetry Power: Writing, Editing, &
Publishing Dynamic Poetry

Photography for Writers: A Writer's
Companion for Image-Making

Flash Writing Series Collection:
A Writer's Companion for Flash Fiction,
Poetry and Image-Making

Table of Contents

For my parents, who introduced me to the library where the universe of information awaited, shelved neatly and card cataloged, and for the internet, the other magical portal of my youth.

Introduction

I've explored and published work in numerous genres throughout my writing career, including short stories, travel essays, a novella, historical fiction, poetry, journalistic articles on numerous subjects, romance, flash fiction, and flash memoir. I have a healthy curiosity about many subjects and styles of prose and poetry, and I've frequently rejected the old saw that a writer should pick a single style or genre rather than dabble. Perish the one-lane mentality!

I'm an enthusiastic, artistic dabbler and encourage that in my students. *Dabbler* is not even the right word—too wishy-washy and lightweight—as a writer sounds for depth and meaning in the writing process. More like *voyager* or *surveyor*. When it comes to the imagination and artistic forms, why limit yourself? Especially before you've even started.

Your inherent curiosity likely drew you to this book. You, too, love to write and have always dreamed of writing a book-length work to share with others. You enjoy researching and networking and sculpting large quantities of information into easier-to-navigate forms. You've probably read a lot of nonfiction and own a shelf of craft books. You, too, have a lot of really cool things to say about a subject that lights you up inside.

Get ready to explore with me one of the most fulfilling forms of nonfiction writing. Writing a reference book can be as marvelously creative and fulfilling as penning a short story, novel, poem, or song.

In this book, we'll dive into an array of ideas ranging from choosing your topic and deciding how you'll divide and organize your book to what kind of tone to take, sustaining your project through unexpected interruptions, deciding whether a traditional press, small press, or self-publishing is the best fit for your book, as well as tips for marketing your literary brainchild, too. Let's get started, shall we?

While I'm very precise and descriptive in this book, offering practical tips and anecdotes about what worked for me and/or my writing students and clients, I want you to keep in mind, even as I give specific advice: leave a little room for serendipity, inexactitude, and surprise.

As you research, write, interview (in some cases), network, get feedback from fellow writers, and edit your book, you may well stumble onto new information and exciting topics related to yours that you had never considered before—grand! That's all part of the process of writing a dynamic nonfiction work. I added six more chapters to this book than my original outline called for, chapters that certainly fleshed out and strengthened the book. As you write what you need to say, you'll expand your range and likely want to share both the new sparks and the old fires with your readers. All the better for your book.

Sure, reference-book writing has the reputation in certain writing circles as being as dry as sawdust—but you and I know otherwise. The process of writing a reference book will strengthen your writing muscles and encourage exciting growth in the style you already possess. Prepare to be amused, challenged, and razzle-dazzled by what you'll discover as you write your reference book—I've felt all three emotions writing every single one of my books, including this one.

So please, take these tips, divided into three helpful sections—Pick and Plan It, Write It!, and Building Your Writing Career: Editing, Pre-Publication, and Marketing—and run forward with the suggestions using *your own* exciting ideas and organizational methods to make your book a distinctive and motivating one for your future readers.

You've got this! Happy voyaging! Write on.

Pick and Plan It

You, the Expert: Adventures in Choosing your Topic

Here's the thing: you're an expert. You might not always feel like it—maybe you can't parallel park or change a tire or program a computer or bake an edible scone that is recognizable as a pastry, but who cares? You don't need to know everything or even *almost* everything to know that you have a lot to say and plentiful personal knowledge on subjects that sparks your interest and your internal fire.

Think all writers who penned sports how-tos or memoirs were professional athletes? Nope. Think all writers who wrote cookbooks were cooking-school-trained chefs? Nein. Think all board game manuals were written by World Scrabble Champions or World Chess Champions? Nyet. Some might be, but most writers who crafted reference books did so *without* blue ribbons or titles or credentials to their name.

Here's the grand thing about writing: unlike rocket science, you don't need to have three advanced degrees to be considered a knowledgeable sharer in your field of interest.

Wanna know how most writers become experts in their chosen topic? Let's take a gander, shall we?

Real-life experience. They love knitting and make one hundred sweaters and twenty-five scarves that they gift others for birthdays. They find sculpting interesting, so they take a class at the local university that soon turns into renting space with other artists that soon turns into a show and a book idea to help other beginning sculptors figure out where and how to share their sculpture with an audience. They start dabbling more seriously in photography, take 2,000 digital photos one summer, break out their film cameras on a lark, and decide to write a book combining their two art forms, photography and writing (okay, disclaimer: this one happened to your author. Check out: *Photography for Writers*). What do these examples have in common? Figure out what you have real-life experience in—this doesn't have to be an academic field of study, such as dentistry or geology (although it could be)—and focus your writing energy on that subject.

They practice the art or the hobby or the topic that they write about. While it's not necessary to be an Olympic hopeful skier or a champion roller-derby skater, if you're going to write a book instructing others on the thrills of either sport, it's certainly helpful to practice the sport. To ski or to skate is to understand the sport from physical, mental, and emotional levels that bring depth to your writing that one just can't get from the sidelines or the cheap seats. Readers will be able to tell if you write a skating reference book but have never skated. Want to know how?

Passion. Experts have enthusiasm and verve for their subject matter. People describing prepping a canvas for painting can make it sound riveting if it's part of their artistic process that revs them to begin their oil paintings, while even the most daring feat of airplane parachuting could be a snooze-fest if the author has no élan for the topic. Do you feel the topic in your gut? Have a rush of elation telling a friend about your latest project or interest? Excellent signs that you approach your topic with the kind of enthusiasm that's infectious and keeps those pages turning.

Conversely, if you notice that Ping-Pong is a recent hot trend, you've just seen three books about Ping-Pong on a top-ten list, and you played it a few times in college—don't, I repeat, *don't*, jump into writing a reference book about it. Problem One: there are already three books on the market about that currently and it's a trend; by the time you finish writing your book, the trend may well pass. Problem Two and the bigger problem: if you're writing with the primary goal of selling and you're not really into the topic (having barely played and long ago), that tepid connection will come across in your writing and likely make a lackluster read. There are millions of readers in the world and just as many, if not more, topics. **Pick a topic that excites you and that you want to learn more about yourself.**

Which brings us to: experts understand that they don't know everything. Right? Let me repeat that in another way: don't pressure yourself into thinking that you have to know everything about your subject *right now, this very minute, before beginning to write.* Nope! Not so.

I knew a sizeable chunk about photography before writing my reference book about it (I've been photographing since I was a teen, had a few photographs published, and had taught a class on photography with tips for writers in making better images on the page and on the digital camera screen), but was I a full-time photographer, did I know all of my F-stops and ISO speeds, had I ever shot a wedding or a graduation photo? Negative, not even close, definitely not. But I trusted my communication skills and where I could unearth the information I needed, and you will, too.

You don't have to be *the* authority or the trendsetter, but you do have to know what you're talking about and have a basis of knowledge in your subject matter. Take the self-inventory that follows and then proceed to the chapter (Even Experts Consult Experts: or, Why You're Gonna Need a Check-up) where we'll explore some handy advice for filling in gaps of knowledge.

You, the Expert: An Inventory

These questions are designed to zero in on your natural interests and areas of expertise. Grab a blank document or a piece of paper and answer each question honestly. Set a timer for fifteen or twenty minutes and move through them intuitively and with as much detail that rises to the surface.

Save your responses and revisit your answers when working through the *Write It!* section. Some of your answers will likely provide inspiration for chapters and topics to explore in your book.

Part One

List three or four hobbies/skillsets/interests you've practiced. First, list hobbies you've practiced in the past year or two. Then, broaden it to hobbies you haven't practiced as recently but still have a strong interest in. Perhaps you had a telescope and are still interested in constellations and planets and sky watching.

What aspects of the listed hobbies/skillsets/ interests do you most connect with? That is, list three or four qualities that excite you about each hobby or interest.

What *don't* you know about these hobbies/ skillsets/interests that you'd love to know? Jot a question or two for each one. If more questions arise, jot those, too. Feel free to keep adding to your list another day.

What aspects of your listed topics do you have *no* interest in exploring or sharing? Perhaps these are areas that are much-talked-about and covered so often as to seem boring or redundant.

Part Two

Choose one topic from your list. Note all of the experiences you've had with this topic, from the tiniest to the most longstanding. For example: maybe you started to cook soup at age four, then by age nine you made your own soup recipes, then by age fifteen you started a soup fundraiser to make money for your favorite charity, and then by thirty-two you made soup for your children and taught them the art of soup's variety. No memory too small or large. The point of this free-writing exercise is to bring up the highs, lows, and in-betweens of your potential topic and to remind ourselves we know a lot more about our topic than we could have imagined at first glance!

If your list for this one topic looks skimpy or uninspiring, no worries. Repeat the process with another hobby or interest from your list. You'll strike pay dirt before too long. One topic will call out to you above the others.

Part Three

Conduct a search at your favorite online book-seller and via Google to see what topics exist for your chosen topic(s). After perusing a few of the books and/or links, answer the following questions:

- What kinds of topics or aspects about the hobby or interest does each book cover? Perusing tables of contents and indexes or glossaries will often provide substantial hints about content.

- What topics are the published books missing that you could address in your book?

- Who seems to be the main audience for the published books?

- What audience are the already-published books on your topic overlooking that you could address?

Part Four, aka: the Bonus Round, Consult your Brain Trust

Waaaaay back in the 1930s and 1940s, US President Franklin D. Roosevelt kept a group of trusted advisors nearby that he called his Brain Trust. He consulted this intelligent faction on matters of national and international policy as well as personal business. They provided suggestions and different angles to complicated problems and proved that two, three, or even ten minds brainstorming can truly be better than one sometimes. We all (informally) have a Brain Trust handy. Text or call a close friend—a trusted writing pal or longtime friend who can be both constructive and encouraging. (Skip the frenemies or passive-aggressives here.) Share your three or four topic options, and then ask what they think your skills are within any of these possible topics. The friend might also have additional insight into the topic or even remember some of the experiences and talents you have relating to the topic that you've forgotten. When I was writing my outline of topics for this book, I bounced my initial table of contents that I'd made with a close writing friend in Michigan who suggested three or four excellent topics that I wouldn't have thought of and which expanded this book in wonderful directions.

Plotter, Pantser, or Plantser?
A Self-Quiz

This quick series of questions will help you determine if you're a plotter, a pantser, or a plantser (a goofy term that indicates a mixture approach).

A plotter creates a sizeable amount of pre-writing *before* writing any of the book, whether planning translates to one outline or several, a collage, webbing a chapter idea, bullet journaling, an audio or video file of topics, or other methods. Plotters believe in having a map prepared and knowing the destination prior to setting out on the journey. On the other hand, panters set out immediately; they free-write with little or no pre-writing to see where the road of their ideas leads on the page. They often write more material than necessary, and then later narrow, omit, collate, shuffle, recombine, add new material, and organize their manuscript *after* trying out the material through writing prose passages or whole chapters to see how pieces fit (or don't fit) together. In between these two opposite approaches to drafting is the plantser.

Plantsers may make a short set of notes for the first chapter or two or create an outline for one section before drafting, but they remain highly malleable between the writing and the planning stages and may flip back and forth between planning and drafting for much, if not all, of the writing process. There's no right or wrong method, and many writers might change from one category to another based on the needs of each project or even each chapter.

These questions might also point the way to deciding whether writing your entire reference book before submitting sample chapters and/or an outline method is for you or if creating a very detailed outline and then writing most of your manuscript once your nonfiction book has been accepted is a practical working method for you.

After taking the quiz, read the coordinating chapter which describes more about each of the approaches.

1. When I first get an idea, I mostly likely:

a. Immediately grab my journal or a computer document and write free-form ideas or an outline. I wouldn't want any of the details to disappear on me!

b. Let it simmer. No hurry to get anything onto paper. Ideas need a few days or weeks to get going, and the ideas will be better if I hold off a bit to see what shows up over time.

c. Mull it over for a day or two and then begin a free-write.

d. Mull it over for a week or few weeks and then make an outline or list details.

2. When I *start* a new project, one of my *favorite* parts is:

a. Thinking about how various themes and ideas connect.

b. The way one detail leads to the next and the next, almost as if by magic, once I start writing them down or talking about them.

c. It varies based on the project.

d. It varies based on how I feel each day when I'm writing and other factors, such as how much or little time I have to write each week so that I connect with the material in a different way each time I write.

3. When I have a new project going, my writing sessions each week tend to:

a. Grow more frequent or longer. Gotta strike while the iron is hot! Leap in and get writing!

b. Surprise me. I might write two or three times one week and then just once the next week, but no worries and no hurry. The writing will flow as it's meant to over time.

c. Vary based on my schedule and other obligations in my personal life. Sometimes, it's just impossible to write for longer than an hour once or twice a week. I have a social life, after all!

d. Vary based on how I feel that week. Some days the ideas come easily while other days, it's like *whose book is this anyway?*

4. **When I'm working on a project, my *least* favorite part is:**

a. Deciding which section or chapter to write first before I have enough ideas.

b. Deciding what to write after I've finished the first chapter(s) or section(s). I get muddled in the middle a lot.

c. It varies by project.

d. It varies based on whether I think the project still has merit after I've worked on it for a few days or weeks.

5. **Ideally, when I'm working on a book or project:**

a. I have a general idea of the arc or content of each chapter or section and probably also have a few ideas for the next book, too. The more ideas the merrier! Bring it on.

b. I like to focus on just one or two ideas or themes at a time until I've perfected and fully explored what I most want to say. Refining my ideas on a micro level is part of the fun of a project. There's plenty of time to explore other content later.

c. Sometimes, I start with one section but then get ideas for another section or chapter, and I must write it down before I forget it. Jumping around, as needed, is all a part of the writing process.

d. Sometimes, I like to focus on one chapter or section at a time, but other times I get bored or unsure of how to finish the section I'm working on, so I take a break and go back to my outline or pre-writing notes to write something else until I figure out the best way to finish my original chapter or section.

6. My feelings about deadlines are most accurately described as:

a. Love 'em! I eat deadlines for breakfast. It's how I get things done.

b. Ugh. They kill the joy of the process, and really, aren't deadlines made to be broken? The muse doesn't work that way—at least, mine doesn't!

c. Meh. They're not fun, but they're necessary.

d. Sometimes I meet deadlines; sometimes I just need more time. Either way is fine.

If you answered mostly a. you are most frequently a plotter. If you answered mostly b. you're often a pantser. If you answered mostly c. and/or d. (or a combination of mostly a. and b.), you likely are a plantser.

It's not an exact science, but knowing your general work habits and views on approaching a topic can inform any modifications you might want to make to your workflow and also inspire your continued writing process.

The Whole Enchilada or a Sliver of the Pie

Now that we've explored a bit about pantsers and plotters (and the in-between plantser option), and you've taken the self-quiz, let's delve in more deeply and take a closer look at which method might best fit your writing process.

Pansters jump in with little or no pre-writing and write away, chopping large swathes of material in the editing phase. Plotters do the opposite—listing, outlining, and using other methods to organize what they want to say *before* they delve in to writing chapters or sections.

I often joke with my students that, while I slightly lean towards being a pantser in chasing my ideas, in my writing practice I'm more closely a hybrid: a plantser. When I sat down to write this book, for instance, I had a few ideas swirling in my mind that I made into a typed outline before choosing the first chapter I wanted to write (which, by the way, wasn't the current first chapter of this book—always stay open to serendipity and to pieces of your book appearing out of order; you can always shuffle them around later—readers will never know which ideas came first in your first draft, unless you tell them, as I just did).

Another way to think of this process: are you a big-picture creator or a little-picture creator? Or perhaps your method flits somewhere in between. Whichever way, there's a great method for writing your craft book.

Big-picture creators tend to want to know their entire list of topics (or many of them) before sitting down to write a chapter or two. Little-picture creators tend to be very detail-oriented and zero in on one very specific topic or theme that they explore at length before zooming out to the content of other chapters or themes.

Whether you tend to be big-picture, little-picture, or somewhere in-between (like your author), this chapter will explore methods and tips for success in approaching the development of a book-length project.

Realize that everyone starts somewhere. Some authors jump in wholeheartedly to outline or prepare to pen a whole book on their topic at once, which is what this book is mostly geared towards. At the same time, you might find it very useful (and a time-saver initially) to explore your topic at first by writing an article or two on your topic to test the waters and/or to build your publication credits in your subject field. The latter method has the advantage of putting less pressure on having enough material to fill a large manuscript and will offer insight into whether this topic or another one would be better to explore for a large, many-month project. The former method of penning the whole book at once matches the verve of writers with big-picture thinking and who might already have written other books (even in other genres) and know that they have more than enough to say on their topic. Either method works, depending on your level of writing experience and the amount of knowledge you already possess or can research about your chosen topic.

Down to the real nitty-gritty: to plan and go, or to go and then adjust the plan? Write it all first...or don't. Plan it all first...and then write some. While the rule of thumb is that you must draft and edit e novels before submitting, editors and agents of nonfiction often expect book proposals and/or submissions where you write and edit two or three sample chapters and/or a detailed or annotated outline but not the whole book. You will write the rest of the book after the acceptance and turn it in weeks or months later based on a date spelled out on the contract.

The pros and cons of writing the book later depend on your own discipline with writing regularly, your personality

(i.e., Do you thrive under the pressure of someone else's deadline or prefer setting your own pace?), and your writing habits and goals. Writing just a few sample chapters and presenting a detailed outline has the advantage of saving you months (maybe years) of working on a manuscript that no one agrees to publish right away. It also gives you the advantage of having materials ready to submit much faster than if you write and polish an entire draft of your nonfiction book. On the flip side, there's the challenging matter of tone. It can be hard (read: a giant headache) to get back into the frame of mind and exact tone to write the remaining chapters after many months have lapsed between submitting initial materials and getting interest from a publisher. This can sometimes lead to days or weeks of uneven chapters that might get shelved before a routine back into the project presents itself. Also, once you have a contract to finish writing something based on a few ideas and/or an outline and sample chapters, there's greater pressure to write the rest of the book not on your own timeline (which can be adjusted easily) but on your editors' or publishers' timelines, which can be a buzz-kill to creativity.

If you're the kind of person who likes writing for the discovery or someone who doesn't set aside several times per week to make consistent progress on your manu-

script, writing under the pressure cooker of a contract might be a painful process. Ditto if you're a frequent polisher of a single chapter before moving on to a new one. I recommend to my writing students and editing clients that they write as much of their books as they can while the ideas are hot. You don't have to show all of your work when you submit (and if the work is unedited or first drafts, you probably shouldn't), but just having the extra material to sculpt, mold, and add to later can be very heartening and helpful in shaping your book in the long run. So sayeth your author, a born lister *and* free-writer; I save many drafts and even my scrap piles from every project I'm working on, just in case. Often, that extra material replaces so-so or downright blah passages later in my writing or editing process. I save great-but-unused passages in separate files that I mark with the date in the document name and on the file itself. I often note at the top of the document both the name of the project that the passage originated from and that the writing is up for grabs at a later time. This system helps me keep track of the information and makes it easy to find again on my computer. There are many other ways to organize these passages. For example, some writers create a single file on their computer, give it a title such as Scraps or Good Phrases, and then anytime they have a passage they wanted to use but can't, they stop by and add to the file. Simple as that. **In my opinion, having more passages to choose from, in order to send the best sample chapters possible, is a more relaxing, more unhurried position for an author to take.**

Then again, choosing your work-flow method really does depend on each writer's lifestyle, motivation level, skill level, and personality. I have plenty of writing friends who harness the publisher's deadline as a sprinter at the starting line, turning out beautifully written books that inspire readers and writing to deadline; I would be a nervous wreck. Even when I wrote this book to deadline, I started writing the very day I signed the contract (and outlined my chapters before then) so that I would have plenty of wiggle-room time in case my muse decided to pack up and flee for several weeks. That never happened, but you never know, and I always leave some extra space in my schedule for the what-ifs (illness, a bevy of freelance work, contest judging, travel) that inevitably present themselves mid-project, whether I write the entire book first (as I often do) or write to editors'/publishers' deadlines (as I did with this book).

I also want to encourage you about organization. Choosing one method doesn't preclude dabbling in the other. It's not an all-or-nothing proposition to write a reference book. You can switch up your

planning and writing stages, flip-flopping, and/or adding more details and ideas to pre-writing plans at any time. Of course, there's always a third possible option for writing a reference book. In-between, makers might combine some techniques of both big-picture and little-picture methods (perhaps beginning a list of four or five topics before sitting down to write a section or chapter to see how it goes and then adjusting the list, adding or taking away from it) depending on the writing process. Or they might write just one or two chapters before returning to their list of topics to add more ideas for future exploration.

Even Experts Consult Experts: or, Why You're Gonna Need a Check-up

I'm embarrassed to say that I almost didn't attend one of the most-encouraging author talks of my life because watching TV or taking a nap topped my list of favored activities that day. At the time, I was more interested in improving my craft (which, granted, is always important, too) than in making money from my art. Fast forward a decade, and I've since revised that idea to give credence to both elements of writing.

I ended up attending the guest-speaker seminar that day because 1. It was free (thank you, generous authors at readings for sharing your knowledge!), 2. I had a rare afternoon off from teaching, and 3. I had author friends attending who knew I could watch TV, read, or sleep anytime (thank you, positive peer pressure!).

At the discussion, the author gave a presentation about pitching article and book ideas to publishers.

Let's call her Jayne because my memory forgets her first name—my bad! Apologies to this generous speaker—but handily remembers her wise suggestions that I began applying that day. Jayne told us her most lucrative writing gigs (writing for parent-themed publications) arose out of a field she was in no way a self-proclaimed expert in at the time—or at least, she didn't think she knew much about writing for an audience with young children.

Here's what happened: she had a toddler son who, the pediatrician said, needed special corrective glasses. As any caring mother, she immediately set up an appointment with an optometrist who the pediatrician's office suggested and had the child fitted for these special lenses. The problem was that there were three or four different brands and styles of these glasses and the salesperson at the optometrist's office was putting the pressure on, big time, that if she chose the least-expensive brand her child might not see as well as he possibly could. As a freelance journalist and a single mother without a money tree growing in her backyard, she felt the tug of guilt and finances in a Colosseum-style double-whammy duel.

What to do? Buy the good-enough glasses and have them break or, far worse, always wonder if she was stunting her kid's development? Buy the mid-range but still ridiculously-priced package? Or pony up for the priciest of the glasses without knowing if they were any more efficient or durable than the lower-costing corrective glasses?

Jayne went with the option she could afford, but the question niggled at her for weeks and weeks afterward. (Her son, by the way, was a healthy seventeen-year-old when I met her; he ran track, swam, and had won a camp prize for archery, so the pair of glasses she chose—and his vision—turned out just fine.)

Out of this experience, she pitched an article investigating her dilemma for other parents going through similar medical-related, child-health conundrums. A national glossy magazine picked up that article, who then asked if she'd be interested in pitching more articles on what they considered common parent challenges that combined research with real-life experience.

I paraphrase, but her response was something like: "You betcha! Here are five more possible ideas from what has happened with my son in the past six months since I sent you that article pitch. I'd be happy to write about any or all of them."

Before long, she knew her editors on a first-name basis and didn't have to keep pitching—they kept coming to her doorstep/inbox asking for more content that she had the freedom to suggest. More often than not, that magazine or another parent-based publication accepted and published her articles. She became a leader in this unexpected-to-her subject and she later wrote a book within her field.

Yeah, sometimes we pick the topic, but other times the topic chooses us. Did Jayne set out to become a leading writer in the field of parenting-themed writing? Never. But this niche was something that she was passionate about, something she grappled with and researched as a writer and as a mom, as well as something that kept pace with her life as her son continued growing alongside her growing readership.

What can we take away from Jayne's experiences?

Jayne was prepared when promising material presented itself in her life. She was open to topics that interested her and didn't discount any of her interests as not worthy of writing down. She didn't say to herself, "This is a boring topic for most people." Or "But I mostly write about the local music scene, and this article won't fit that topic at all. Who would read this, anyway?" The eyeglass idea itched at her mind, and she recognized that feeling as topic gold. (Coincidentally, the case could be made that her article turned into a paycheck later, a different but equally agreeable form of coin.)

Jayne was not intimidated by what she didn't know: she examined her questions to find out what she needed to learn, as well as

what her target audience would find most helpful. Jayne never said, "This eyeglass thing is important to me, but I'm only one mother and some of my readers don't even have kids. Besides, maybe somebody else would disagree with the choice I made." No, Jayne knew that if *she* lost sleep over the eyeglass decision, there would be many, many others who also would wonder related questions about their kids' lives. So, although Jayne didn't immediately set up a website and declare herself a leading authority in child health or family journalism, her work dovetailed into both areas and built over time to demonstrate her knowledge and interest in both fields.

Experts show initiative, as did Jayne. They realize what they don't know and aren't afraid to spend time and effort seeking it out. In her talk, Jayne was the first person to admit that: *I'm not a pediatrician or nurse or healthcare professional, and I wasn't even on the family-issues beat before the eyeglass article. But I am a writer, and I know how to find out anything I don't know, either through others' first-hand experience or their written sources or both.*

Which leads me to: **Jayne took action to round out her knowledge base. She interviewed with the finesse and skill of a ninja.** She not only jotted notes on areas she didn't know a lot about but wanted to, but she also made a list and looked up several people she wanted to interview, emailed them to introduce herself, and shared clips/links to her published writing so that these strangers would see her professionalism and her writing style. She then conducted interviews with those who replied to her interest in talking with them. Some of Jayne's interviewees didn't want to be named while others were happy to be on the record in her writing, but it didn't matter, either way— Jayne broadened her knowledge base and gleaned even more ideas for her writing from these interviews, a big win for her and for her writing.

Jayne had a pluck and go get 'em attitude; she was determined. No setbacks stopped her writing. She told us fellow writers at her talk that she needed to write the article about her son so much that, although she sent short pitches to the first magazine, she was prepared to go down a list of eight or ten publications until she found the magazine that would publish what she wanted to write. What if no magazines had calls for the subject she wanted to write? No biggie: she'd just sit down and research and write the article for the sheer pleasure of figuring out the many facets of why the eyeglass debacle struck so many chords and pushed so many buttons for her. Then, she would research other markets and pitch the article idea again to different venues that had similar content or readership but perhaps hadn't published about this topic yet. She was reasonably sure someone else would enjoy her topic and completely believed that she'd find a publisher eventually for her ideas. She was absolutely right. **Additional meaningful takeaways on double-taking and getting outside assistance:**

Speaking of which, it's worth noting that every writer has pockets of missing knowledge where they could brush up or add to what they already know—**yes, you'll research some when you write a reference book, no matter how much insider knowledge you already have on your subject.** The last thing you want is to look like a newbie or to get your facts crossed when presenting yourself as a leader in the field.

The researching and editing processes include fact-checking, double-checking details or statistics, and/or checking attributions for quotes.

Where will you look? The internet, sure. Google is a place to start but do an advanced search and check more than one search engine. But please: *don't* stop there.

Reference librarians, school librarians, librarians period are an amazing resource of information: consult them at your favorite local library or a campus near you.

The Brain Trust. Remember that small group of pals we mentioned earlier? Text or email a few who have knowledge in your field. It can't hurt. What slips through one person's mind like a sieve, two or three others recall with absolute clarity.

Teachers/instructors for the win. Know some knowledgeable teachers within the field you're writing about? Reach out. Many professors and educators are detail-oriented and possess a wealth of knowledge. Also, they tend to be pretty responsible and want to connect correct information with curious minds, so if they don't know the answer to your quandary, they'll likely search to see if they can find a resource for you. However, keep in mind that they are busy with their own students, so do be patient about their response times.

Editors. Yes, you'll need one and might want two: one to proofread and fact-check your copy and another for developmental editing to make sure that you have fleshed out your ideas clearly and well.

If you pitch a book to be published, you'll likely be assigned one or two of these glorious professionals as part of your contract—congrats! The free-to-you services these editors offer you are impressive and will save you from numerous embarrassing gaffes that could have made reader cringe and cause them to post negative online reviews of your book.

Self-publishing? No worries and good news: there are plenty of freelance editors

you can hire for varying rates to fact-check and proof your work, saving you numerous headaches and the heartache of not being able to spot your own gaffes. They are well worth their money.

Try this exercise:

Write for fifteen minutes about aspects of your topic that you aren't sure about or could learn more about. Then, hop online to begin researching after making a list of two or three experts you could reach out to and/or interview.

Pro tips for this exercise: Great news! Most leaders in their fields have websites with information about how you could reach out to them directly. Easy-peasy! If you don't know these experts personally, approach with the following guidelines of respectful initial contact.

• **Keep your initial message very brief.** Write one or two sentences about your project. Include links to your website and/or social media and/or possibly a short piece or excerpt from your project or other published work. Inquire if they might be interested in answering a few short questions about your subject.

• **Make sure to include your full contact information**, including your email and phone number.

- **Don't be upset or take it personally if you never hear back from them**. This has happened to me, too. It's a bummer, but it happens. Next!

  - If you don't hear back in two or three weeks, **research another knowledgeable potential interviewee.** There are plenty of people who'd love to share what they know—don't let a non-responder or two get you down. You've got this!

An extra pro tip, just for you, fellow pro: Remember what I said earlier about the value of librarians? Three cheers for these supportive folks. Now, off you go to your local library or college or institution of higher learning to consult one of these fabulous purveyors of plenteous facts. They can suggest not only books and periodicals but also online resources and possibly even the names of those you might not have imagined researching or contacting.

No Envy Goggles, or: There's Already a Book about My Topic

After turning forty, I started to notice something about my life experiences thus far: patterns. There were a lot of people and events that had cycled through my life from early years, laid low for months or even years until I thought them gone forever, *no mas*!, and then whammo! There they were again, knocking on my proverbial door or presenting another opportunity for growth. Usually, they reappeared during a period of change or doubt to uplift my thoughts and buoy my confidence on days when I needed it or to show me just how far I've traveled emotionally and intellectually in preceding years based on the compassion or closure I could now offer.

Over the years, I've learned not to burn bridges completely with anybody or anything if possible from these cycles. You just never know when a memory will turn back up or around to teach you something, and I want to stay open and cautiously optimistic. By now, I know myself quite well enough to set boundaries and know what a rotten deal feels like. Progress! The gift of cycles!

And I know I'm certainly not alone in noticing this phenomenon of flow. It's like this for everyone in certain stages of our lives or at special times of the year, like holidays. The elementary school friend you haven't seen or talked to in years who looks you up and private messages you. The little inkling you had four years ago to learn how to make and can your own pasta sauce; you were too busy, yet the saucy seed of that idea doesn't completely die. A friend mentions his new canner three months ago, and then someone asks what you want for your birthday next month, and the canner idea reappears from your brain for no apparent reason. The time's right for you to grab those tomatoes and get your sauce popping.

Timing. Timing is the key to a lot of connections and projects in our lives.

Here's something that sometimes scares my writing clients and students and, to be truthful, it's something to think about but not something to stop us in our book-writing at all: *there are already books out there about my topic.* Maybe even a lot of them.

I hear you. There were already books about flash fiction before I wrote one. Ditto with poetry. And a myriad of creative nonfiction essays and books. And there will be books about all three of these subjects long after, too.

I welcome it now, but before I wrote my first nonfiction series, I'd already spent my thirties (pause on that for a second: a ten-*year* period) hearing students toss me affirmations that I demurred. Things like, "You sure know a lot about that topic." Or "Ever thought about writing a book about it?" or "It makes so much sense the way you put it. You need to share that with more writers." Or "You make me feel like I can do it, too. You should post that on your blog." The latter of which I always responded with: "Oh, I don't have a blog. Well, not yet, maybe not ever, but I'll ponder that and keep it in mind." The suggestions about the book-writing were a lovely ego stroke, in the nicest way, and made me thrilled as a communicator, but I wasn't in a place of enough confidence to dream about pursuing writing the books in a practical sense. Not yet.

I was still learning myself, I reasoned. I was very busy teaching, which was true. But I will also share candidly that (based on wish lists online and my own sagging bookshelves of writing texts) the fact that there are *so* many nonfiction books about writing already out there daunted me.

Yes, you heard that correctly—your can-do, enthusiastic author was intimidated and closed down shop before I'd begun thinking of writing these books. Who, me?

Even with the many signs in my life along the way that doubled as flaming arrows for the projects, I ignored writing projects which were exactly the *right* projects for me. I patiently pushed aside the positive reinforcement from writing students. For pitifully long.

That wasn't new, I'm sad to say.

For instance, when I was a senior in college and writing an honors thesis, I chose the topic: Women Writers and the Writing Process. Yes, I was writing about writing even in 1999 (how meta!). Even then, I had a passion for conveying ideas about the writing process and a clear sense of identity: a writer, even if nothing was getting published yet and I didn't have a writing community yet.

Back then, I found three books on creative writing and some articles on microfiche machines that I paid to photocopy pages from at the campus library. There wasn't a ton to choose from yet in the form of craft or writing-related reference books. There was Natalie Goldberg's pivotal *Writing Down the Bones* (which I still adore; I own multiple copies and have gifted copies to writing friends, too) and Anne Lamott's ever-inspiring *Bird by Bird*. And then, I'm embarrassed to say, there was a third book I borrowed via interlibrary loan that had a giant pencil sketched on the cover. (My sincere apologies to the author of this book whose title and author I've completely forgotten—I gleaned useful knowledge and encouragement from it for my thesis, so my props to you.)

During my first few years of teaching, this slim cadre of craft books exploded exponentially as more and more writers added exciting nonfiction how-tos specifically aimed at various genres. Since I was a working writer, my collection began not only to include the genres I wrote myself (mainly poetry and fiction at that time) but also reference books about genres my students were interested in writing, such as flash, graphic novels, and personal essay writing.

Then, the digital publishing revolution happened, with the e-book explosion, around 2010. Many big bookstore chains and local bookshops with character (sadly) closed at that time. Several chunks were taken out of my heart when my local bookshop put up their going-out-of-business sign. The day I browsed close-outs and saw they were selling even the almost-empty shelves was a doomy day indeed.

Much as that was such a loss of atmosphere and coziness while browsing, I'm enough of a pragmatist and glass-half-full person to see the flip side: abundant promising opportunity for writers. With the rise of online book retailers and electronic publishing getting easier and easier, small presses and self-publishing writers now have an entire world as an audience at the touch of a few buttons. Magic! Endless prospects for publication and a strong readership!

While I'm still much more of a tactile-book creature, the ebooks I own save space (which I sorely need) and are marvelously instant. Where books sometimes took weeks to get from the library or the brick-and-mortar bookstores, I can now browse thousands of titles in minutes and, usually in two days, have the print copy in my hands. Or a few seconds if I buy an e-book. Also a benefit as an author: digital sales are a significant income stream, in addition to print copies. *Vive la révolution!*

Okay, fine, you might be thinking, *but what does any of this have to do with me and my book and the fact that there's a dispiriting number of reference titles out there already that share my topic?*

Great question. **If, like me, you receive signs that writing a book is something you would very much like to do and find meaningful, then no matter how many books are out there on your topic, you owe it to yourself to write *your* reference book. I truly believe that there will never be too many books on any one topic and that there's not time enough to be envious of how another author created their book.** You've got your own book to write!

Just because a lot of other people have already imparted wisdom doesn't mean that you don't have insights of your own to share. There's a book-buying market eager

for more books, even on similar topics or themes.

Nobody says: you know what, there are just a ridiculous amount of science fiction and fantasy books, so who needs another one? And romance? That genre is SO done! No, these genres are top sellers with loyal fan bases for specific authors and characters and sub-genres. Readers are hungry for more and more pages.

Approach the process of writing your reference book with an expansive mindset. There are never too many books in *any* genre because your book will contain what their book doesn't or will say it in a way that is as individual to you as your fingerprints.

There's room for everybody, and always one more, at the book-crafting table. I'm a firm believer in nudges and signs. I'm also a believer in the right timing. **This chapter is your sign; you've probably had others. Don't wait years like I did. Begin.**

Try this exercise:

Read at least three or four books in your genre. See what's out there and already published in your topic, and then start making a list of what is either missing *or* of what you'd like to cover in a different way than the other books on your same topic.

On Books and Sweet Inspiration

Disclaimer: this is the airy-fairyiest, pep-talkiest chapter of the book. If you're a die-hard realist or a skeptic, I'll admit up front that there's not much for you in this one—kindly proceed to the next chapter.

For the rest of us: *bienvenue* and welcome! I've been awaiting your arrival.

Most of us who are bookworms have found that books have an inherent magic to them. Even though being a writer today doesn't carry quite the same cultural cache that it might have before the era of the internet, movies, and TV, let's face it: it's still pretty dang impressive to most people to hear that a person is writing, or has written, one. Why is this?

What is it about writing books, and how can we harness a little (or a lot!) of this razzle-dazzle to carry forward to our readers?

Books are more than just a single story. They are first of all objects with thematic elements in their titles and thematic art—every book has a cover, whether or not they are paperback or entirely electronic onscreen.

Yeah, yeah. Still, **what is it that we hope to tap into when we decide to write a book?**

- Books contain our history and our visions.

- Books explore vitally important subjects to us, not just as individuals but often also as cultures and subcultures.

- Books reflect our struggles and biases and shortcomings and strengths amidst almost impossible circumstances.

- Books suggest change is not only possible but inevitable.

- Books raise questions that we may or may not be comfortable voicing verbally.

- Books educate and challenge our preconceptions.

- Books are entertaining. They may not be the fastest or most visual of entertainment, but they are still endlessly riveting and have the power to reveal new and intriguing details upon rereading months or even years later.

- Books are a form of rapid escape. Okay, so technically this might go along with entertainment, but what I'm focusing more on here is the uplifting, transporting, immediate get-out-of-jail-free card that comes from dropping into a book on a quiet Sunday afternoon's mind travel.

- Books are inexpensive compared to the endless hours their authors lovingly pour into their creation.

- Books are portable and a friend for troubled or isolated times.

- Books hold a mirror to what we love and value as well as what we don't but maybe should.

- Books are collectable and shareable, both via discussion verbally and online as well as handed down to friends or family and gifted for special occasions.

- Books are readily available and, now more than ever, findable and dispersible at the touch of a button or two on everyone's phones.

Okay, so there are myriad more attributes I had a yen to list above, but we all get the idea. **Writing a book can easily become your legacy** to present to future readers, to your kids and grandkids and nieces/nephews/niblings, even to your former young self who aspired to be a writer way back in elementary or middle school.

Writing a book is a worthwhile, inherently meaningful pursuit to invest your precious life into because books are inherently meaningful and worthwhile to our development as people on intellectual, emotional, and spiritual levels.

As such, please oh pretty please with a cherry on top, pick a subject you have passion about, a subject that makes you wonder and that might just keep you up at night, a subject that makes you eager to fall down the rabbit hole to find endless more discoveries about your topic, a subject that tickles your funny bone or makes you weep, a topic that makes you want to run out and tell your bestie why you care about this topic and the latest facts or anecdotes or tidbits you just wrote about.

That kind of subject will be a gift to your readers and a gift to yourself, making the writing and editing processes a journey you just might be eager to take many, many times in your manuscripts.

That's the kind of book you owe it to yourself to write—not the latest trendy subject everyone's writing about this year. Not the "guaranteed-to-sell" book (although good luck anticipating that). Not a subject that's good enough but that bogs you down and makes you yawn halfway through writing it. Not the book your mom, coworker/boss, friend, or spouse told you that you should write. Not the book someone else asks you to write about their experiences because they're not a writer themselves. No. The book *you* want to write about the subject that tugs at your sleeves and keeps tugging is the book you should write. Any other "good-enough" topic just isn't.

When you write a book on a subject you have a passion for, it will show to your readers and spark their own imaginations to their own discoveries—ultimately, that's what writers want. Yet another magical element of writing a book and being this most mystic of artists, the writer, is this connection between what sparks you and your readers.

It's not an easy pursuit to write a book, and there will be plenty of setbacks and run-arounds and challenges, but it's certainly a vital and valuable pursuit. Just make sure you're pursuing something that you truly love, and then love it without turning back.

Try this exercise:

Set a timer for ten or fifteen minutes and write about one or all of the following questions:

- What do books mean to you and your life? Feel free to start your own list or to use some of the starting ideas I included in this chapter about what books have meant to me.

- What are the top three traits of your subject that attract you to write about this topic?

- What books inspired you to be a writer? What nonfiction books, in particular, inspire your writing? If you don't have any, start reading nonfiction craft books more widely to see the kinds of tones and subject matter already out there that will inspire you further.

This is meant to be a breezy, off-the-top-of-your-head exercise to encourage your passion for your subject. Don't stop to edit or rewrite the list. Don't write what someone else has said they like about your writing. This one's all about you and your relationship to books and writing.

Enjoy, and please—if the timer goes off and you're really getting into it, set that timer for fifteen minutes more. I won't tell.

When You Get the Choice: Be All-In

I was reading a personal essay in a magazine this morning (yep, I still subscribe to some ink-and-paper ones), and the author described how his father influenced his twisting-and-turning career path until he landed on coaching. His candor and passion for his vocation was impressive and practically levitated off the page.

But what impressed me even more was one sentence where he mentioned how disappointed he was with himself when he hadn't met his personal challenges with the decisiveness and determination he'd expected of himself. At these low points, his dad had offered consistent encouragement. He described his dad's care and compassion, not only for his own vocation and community but also for his children's lives, as *all-in*.

I was thunderstruck: *all-in.*

Now, I don't know about you, but I know a boatload of people from all walks of life, social demographics, and backgrounds—it's one of the delights of teaching an art. Many, many people write, to some extent, about their families, their loved ones, and the communities they've made or been a part of. I've read tales of unimaginable pain and grief following abandonment that made me feel such admiration for their perseverance as well as wonder and awe that these people made it out of bed this morning.

I've also gotten emails from people in the midst of heartrending crises—the drug addiction and loss of a sibling, the adoption of a niece/nephew/nibling or grandchild after a horrific car crash, the house that burned in the wildfires or was lost to hurricane waters, the spin-out after a partner's affair. I've learned that everyone has multiple heartaches that they're carrying around at any given time, many of which we never learn about except through their art or when they reach out for compassion in the midst of suffering. This is part of the human condition and part of leading an authentic path. **Our work should aim to connect, not only to our own happiness and struggles, but to the lives of people trying to walk this same artistic path.** This idea reaffirms itself so many times, in my classrooms, in my inboxes, in my relationships.

What I don't reflect on as often, but which impacts my life as a writer just as much, is the upbeat side of fortitude. There are oodles of people in our everyday lives and in our communities who show the kind of self-sacrifice of time and effort that make a quiet difference each day and keep our worlds spinning in subtle yet important ways. Yeah, somebody woke up at 3 a.m., bundled up into the cold darkness, left their still-sleeping children or spouse or dog or feline companion, to put on the coffee pot so you could drive through at five before work to get your hot beverage. It doesn't have to be huge to be impactful.

There are people all around us who are *all-in*. They often blend into the wallpaper, so to speak, because consistency doesn't attention-grab or look all that glamorous. These are the people who are so busy or so giving or so ordinary-seeming that few of us even notice what they've sacrificed and keep sacrificing to support others and themselves.

Look, we all probably know a ton of other people, too, who let their intentions drive the bus. They're half-in, half-out. Lukewarm about their goals and their lives. Fierce and then flaky in turns. Or they scatter themselves among so many possible paths that they exhaust themselves before they hit the midway point. Or they decide they'd rather do something else and that nobody cares about what they're doing anyway.

These are the people who put off the nudges they get to keep practicing their art until they've run out of steam and just don't practice the art much, or at all, anymore. Or ten or twenty years go by before they return to their original goals. Or they share their work only to get bad or luke-warm reactions that turn them off of their path of sharing for long stretches, if not forever. **It's totally understandable. It's also sometimes a mixture of tiredness, self-sabotage, and fear (of success or failure or both).**

Writing a book is a fortitude marathon. Writing *anything* is a long-term prospect, especially when seeking publication. As with raising children or enrolling in a degree program or going up for a work promotion or getting married, the results from your efforts are anything but guaranteed from your investment. There's the very real possibility that you can try and try and try only to get rejected again and again by the very people with whom you hope most to connect. There's the very real possibility something or someone or a lot of somethings will trip you up and derail your best efforts.

There's also the possibility you can keep stepping over and around obstacles and succeed in connecting more than you ever imagined.

The friends, family, clients, and students I admire most are the ones with stick-to-it-iveness. The people who show up when they say they will and keep showing up. Let me repeat that glorious thought for the hope it emanates:

the people who show up when they say they will and keep showing up. May we strive to emulate these people.

The authors whose books we hold, the designers whose clothes we wear, the inventors whose products we use: these people were *all-in*. People who dedicate themselves get things done. They suffer their heartbreaks and gut-sinking doubts and failures aplenty like anybody else, yet they'll rise to try again, even if it's patently foolish. Perhaps *especially* when it's patently foolish. What's the harm in trying? And trying and trying and trying ...

I wrote for years without getting published, spending a ton of time and effort and some would say my most-carefree years of my teens and twenties in a haze of stories, poems, and essays and in classrooms as both a student and a teacher. Although I did some fun traveling and fulfilled my grad-school dream, I admit that I was an introvert who hid out a lot more than I probably should have. Yes, you are talking to the queen of sublimation (just call me Queenie). When romantic connection continued to baffle, riddled with hurdles that overwhelmed and felt the equivalent of a wobbly, punctured tire (still does sometimes!), I kept turning to my known strengths: work and friendship. Two areas guaranteed to produce positive results as long as I kept investing ... and I did. It wasn't until my thirties that I began to realize that turning my back on my underdeveloped skills (and I surely have more than one of those! Hello, parallel parking and sewing and fixing mechanical things and ...) to focus solely on "sure things" would never yield the stronger, happier present I want; what can I say? We're all works in progress.

My point is: as friends got promotions, got mortgages, got family portraits on their mantels, I published for years without earning a dime, redoubling efforts on my occupations to have the money to have the time to write. With no promise or guarantee to make anything from my art. That looks and sounds iffy and even idiotic on paper. But I'm the kind of person who firmly believes in personal investment (financially is a whole different matter since I've had little to invest, but I digress).

I hung in there. Despite disappointments and rainclouds of rejections, there was a rich, inner fulfillment to the struggle and the small successes. Lately, the rewards have been a lot more consistent for my invested literary efforts from this very prolonged period when I gave up a lot of hanging out, luxuries, and movies to pour devotion and vision into my writing. Totally worth it, but I can tell you that it didn't look or sound like a wise investment for many, many years.

Lots of people in my daily life (for good reason) probably still think my path is oddball and I agree: I've not lived a cookie-cutter life professionally or personally. **It looks, and sometimes feels, like a fool's errand. A merry fool, but yeah, definitely not a secure path.**

But it is *my* path to nurture and develop, and we each have one.

Which brings me to envy itself. Look: we all see the highlight reels of our coworkers', neighbors', friends' lives on social media. The tendency to compare has never been stronger or more enticing, especially on our down days when we know that we're not where we want to be with our writing projects or in our personal lives. Meanwhile, so-and-so just celebrated his twentieth anniversary, and such-and-such just lost fifty pounds and went to the Caribbean and what's-his-face quit smoking and got his dream counseling job.

It can be even more intimidating to look up our favorite authors' websites or social media; the temptation to feel lesser about our own projects is punishing.

That should be me, a small part of us might think. *How'd they do that and I'm still struggling?*

You know, there's a flip side to all of this that we don't often consider. People read the highlight reels *you* post for the world. Not only should that encourage us to be gentle and mindful of what we share with the world, but also it's a unique compliment. Hear me out: somewhere out there an acquaintance is jealous of the fact that you're writing, that you're taking positive steps towards your writing goals. Sure, right now you see behind the curtains and know all of your missteps and muddled drafts and rejection slips, but they don't. They see your highlight reel and think you're making it.

Oh, they'll likely never tell you that they're envious, so you'll never know, but they're out there. Actually, be grateful when they *don't* tell you. I've been on the receiving end of that kind of blurted admission, and it's an awkward moment for all involved. I never want to apologize for my hard-earned successes or belittle the obstacles I continue to overcome, but at the same time, I want to honor their sadness, frustration, and disappointment and offer some nugget of encouragement as I've also lived their artistic frustrations. Talk about a minefield!

At its root, **envy is discouragement turned inward**, which is very easy to do as writers. We've all been there. Strive to **take discouragement as a background detail, not a permanent setback that's unique to you.** You want to write this book, and probably others, too. **Also, it can't hurt to limit your time on social media; invest the "extra" to your writing.**

People who have follow-through are remarkable and they eventually get their due and get noticed. Stay in the lane you're in, put blinders on (so to speak), and charge forward.

Whenever possible and as often as possible, show the world you're all-in, do the work, and then sit back and watch the magic multiply before getting back to work again.

Try this exercise:

Write about a person in your life who is all-in. In what ways has that person demonstrated consistency and excellence with not a lot of praise or notice? What sacrifices do you think that person has made to meet their goals and/or to reach out to others?

Bonus points: drop an encouragement text today to this marvelous *all-in* person. You'll cheer them more than you can ever imagine.

Writing a Book: All the Feels, Some of the Reasons

I'm an INFJ (hello, Myers-Briggs!) and a give-it-a-try-why-not? person by nature. I'm also a creative writing teacher, editor, big sister, and freelance writing coach (but you might have already guessed that—I'm so unathletic, it's literally the only "sport" in which I'd dare to call myself a coach). I live to support and boost other authors, and I truly believe that all of our voices and all of our books will enrich the world.

On the other hand, time and experience have tempered my glass-half-full attitude just a tad with a few scratches and nicks on the glass. Enough to know that book-writing, editing, and publishing carry many loaded motives and mixed, concealed expectations that can lead to disappointment in the long run for the author.

It's a great idea right now to consider some of the positive, healthy reasons for writing a craft book while honestly assessing and adjusting expectations on some of the often-hidden, questionable reasons.

Some positive, healthy reasons for writing a book:

You want to share the depth of your knowledge in your favorite field/subject matter. Like teaching, there's something very satisfying, as an author, in sharing the many nuances, challenges, and fulfillments of what it's taken you many months, if not years, to learn. In our everyday lives, we're not always surrounded by many (if any) people who have the same hobbies and passions that we do; writing a book will help you to connect with and find your "people" who share the same passions. Win-win.

You look forward to learning more about your subject. Writing a book is a marvelous process of "now's the time." The process will provide a reason to take the time to research questions you've always had or are still learning the answers to about your subject matter. We're all ever-deepening our knowledge. As Hemingway said: "**We are all apprentices** in a craft where no one ever becomes a master." Use that apprenticeship-style zeal to your advantage.

You have a natural interest and passion for your subject matter.

You love communicating with others in written form. Here's the thing, I'm not the world's best on-the-spot conversationalist in person. I often think of a witty comment a few minutes *after* the conversation has sped on to another subject. Remember that Myers-Briggs reference earlier in this chapter? Yeah, the I stands for Introvert for a reason. On paper, we can refine our thoughts as many times as we need to and at our own pace to communicate clearly and meaningfully (I wrote parts of this paragraph three times—no shame in the game). Often, part of the fulfillment of writing a book includes having epiphanies and aha moments that we add to an earlier chapter as the writing mojo heats up in the drafting stage. This morning (about five weeks into writing this book), I woke with an illustrative example for another chapter running through my mind. I could hardly wait to fire up the draft and write it in, and I grabbed my bedside writing notebook to scratch it onto the page even before I put on my glasses, before the idea took off again!

Writing a book has always interested you.

You feel excited about the many layers of the writing process.

The self-discovery, stress-relief, and fun involved. Writing is a mostly solitary art—at least in the drafting stages—and that's a marvelous thing. You'll spend a large number of weeks all up in your head (in the best possible way), working on refining your book's concept, imagining fitting additions and examples, and experimenting with new ideas as you draft. The closest artistic comparison I can think of is an artist with endless paint tubes, a ginormous palette, and canvases of all shapes and sizes at your disposal, and all you have to do (at that moment) is sit down with your imagination and create! No pressure, no fuss: just playing around to see what you can make and with a far-off end goal: a communicative book. Sweet freedom! Getting a little lost in the labyrinth of cool possibilities often relieves stress and feels pleasant, taking you out of your everyday cares for a few minutes or hours while you write. The craft of writing is its own reasoning and pleasure.

Some questionable/sketchy reasons for writing a book:

Fame. We live in an era of celebrities who get paid beaucoup bucks to post product content and everyday people sharing their talents one minute who become household names the next. If the thrill of the spotlight and becoming a rising hotshot are two reasons that motivate you, consider again. Of all the arts, writer fame—even among authors who are paid speakers with agents and who have published numerous books—doesn't tend to be of the same stratospheric trajectory as in some other arts. There are far, far easier and less time-consuming ways to become a star or a household name or earn the admiration or envy of others than writing.

Reconnection/Missed Connection—AKA: affection, romantic love, or instant healing. This one's a biggie: buckle up, buttercup. It can be an especially gut-wrenching category because it's *not* something we usually associate consciously with our writing. Most writing classes don't discuss realistic and *un*realistic expectations surrounding publishing what we write because there are already endless craft topics to cover. The post-publishing process can seem pretty nebulous and a vague end-goal floating like a cloud on the horizon, leaving imaginations to fill in lots of blanks with far-reaching, sometimes grandiose expectations of what life ABP (After Book Publication) will bring.

Our unrealistic expectations tend to lurk in the background and muddy our motivations and hoped-for outcomes. Adding to this conundrum: we don't tend to express these expectations verbally but hide the possibilities in our private thoughts. We often set ourselves up for disappointment, annoyance, and sorrow inadvertently if we write for some of the following reasons: to prove ourselves worthy, intelligent, creative or cool to people we want to impress, or aspire to change minds about their initially simplistic assessment of us or in hopes of competing with authors we secretly think are more talented than we are, or for earning the attention or compliments of would-be friends, parents, bosses, children's friends, estranged friends, exes, group leaders, or would-be loves/partners/our writing groups.

That said: most of us (your author included) have at one time or another secretly wished our writing would lead to better outcomes in at least one or two of our life connections.

Yet, **you produce resonant writing with a focus on how it helps *others* on the same artistic path, not on possible emotional perks for ourselves.** Eighty percent or more of the time, the people you write for (your book's target audience) *won't* be people you know "in real life" right now (although you might meet some of them at a reading online or in person in the future). As someone who has had a few books published and who helps clients with the publication process, my experience has been more like: a few people may love your book and tell you about it (often people you don't know personally or who you know tangentially; no matter where praise comes from, it's sustaining and welcomed) and some people may hate your book, vocally (these folks might be strangers who haven't published a thing themselves but also might be people you do know in real life using anonymous handles).

But the vast majority of people you know personally in real life won't communicate about your book one way or another—it's a blip in their busy lives. People in this last category generally don't mean it in a bad way: they just have too much going on to make your book the focus of their attention. Understandably. Or there's the outside chance that they could be jealous or annoyed that you made your dream come true and maybe they are still working on theirs, but you'll probably never know it because they say nada about your book, either way. Dust off your feet and move on. It's not an assessment of you or your book.

Even harder to swallow is this advice: There will be no meet-cute story, nor vindication, nor once-in-a-lifetime reunions surrounding most book publications. The hottie from the office or your runners club or your writing group or from your high-school days won't find you more appealing or adorable after reading your book and text you to get coffee sometime. Your frenemy or long-lost friend won't call to say how much they miss you after reading your book (they might stalk your social-media pages and author website, though). If any of these people read your book at all (don't hold your breath but realize that some will), they likely won't mention it. Your estranged siblings or exes won't tout your talent or express sudden under-standing of your point-of-view. The bully from college or your first job won't come groveling with an apology to demonstrate that, in the end, you really were the better person (see "blip in their lives" above). The teacher who told you that maybe you weren't college material (true story) won't email how much they loved your book and were wrong about you. There will be no catharsis from writing your book except that you have met your goal for yourself.

Your book itself is not a ticket to an easier social life. The cricket-chirping silence from huge swathes of people in your personal and professional life after you publish a book may, at first, astonish.

Unlike writers depicted in movies, books don't lead to post-publication happy endings. You still have to keep working—on your writing and on yourself. Writing a book doesn't frequently lead directly to significant others or marriages, nor does it fix crumbling or already-crumbled personal relationships with family or friends or troubled past bullies. In fact, depending on your honesty level, they might escalate the crumbling of said tenuous ties. Expecting (even a very little bit) your book to pave the way for you to either create romance or mend rifted relationships is like having a child with hopes of mending a relationship—an ill-advised idea with high-pressure stakes that most frequently leads to heartache all around. But yeah, plenty of people still go that route, consciously or not.

You will be the same person *after* your book is published as you were *before* and *during* writing your book, with the same

struggles and untapped talents and frustrations—that's both the bad news and the extraordinarily good news (see below).

Writing a book *can, and often does,* bring a sense of self-fulfillment and lead to important life changes in occupation or geographic location and even increased confidence in your own abilities at accomplishing a life goal. Those are huge gains, no doubt about it. Notice that all of these possible outcomes are self-focused and based on your own personal actions.

You have something unique to say. Now, please oh pretty **please: save yourself heaps of misery, and *don't* count on specific actions, verbal or written support, understanding, or positive changes in behavior from people you know or once knew as a result of your book. That's way too much stress to put on a book or on yourself as its author.** If you find yourself feeling this way, talk to a friend or fellow writer or counselor, stat—just voicing the unexpected disappointment and mixed emotions about others' reactions (or lack thereof) helps.

Profits, baby! This one is perhaps the trickiest of all reasons. Hey, we all need money to survive, and to earn from our writing is a reward that frequently arrives after years of giving the prose away for free to build an audience. So, what's so bad about monetizing this time?

Nothing at all! Some of my favorite days are when my royalty checks arrive (now more likely to be "royalty direct deposits"). I even recall taking a few photos of my first royalty checks before cashing them back in the day to prolong the satisfying feeling of accomplishment.

Before you think of me as a giant hypocrite: the *problem* with profits comes when they are your *primary or sole* motivation for writing books.

I've known many writers who were, at first, bummed when their royalty checks didn't earn enough for them to pare back hours at their day job or stop freelancing or quit. Expecting to publish and financially live off of a single book's royalties, or even multiple books, is unrealistic for most writers and about as likely as living off of your lottery winnings: it's technically possible, but the odds make it extraordinarily unlikely. I know countless published authors; the majority of us don't live off of our royalty checks or scale back on other employment, alas!

I advise *not* quitting or scaling back your hours at your day job(s) for a while, at least for the duration it takes you to write and publish a first book and to get the first few royalty checks to assess estimated profits per year. Royalty checks can vary vastly from payout to payout as well as from book to book. Putting financial pressure on yourself as you write a book invites burn-out and disappointment and maybe even abandoning your writing dreams forever (I've seen that happen and I don't want to have it happen to any others).

Whether you self-publish or publish with an indie publisher or get an agent and publish with a traditional publisher, **gleaning profits from your writing career will be a slow-building, marathon-style element of your career: that's the one hundred percent normal route for authors. Take the long view of slowly-accruing net profits for many, many months, if not years, as a supplemental income stream rather than counting on cashing in now.**

Personally, it's my teaching, freelance editing, and work with writing clients that pay the cable bill. I view my book royalties as either money to invest back into my books, advertising them to gather more readers, or to buy myself a little treat to celebrate my latest book making its way into the world. I bought myself a bottle of fancy French perfume with one royalty check that I'd never otherwise splurge on, and each time I wear it I recall, with a smile, the care I invested in my book as well as the book-release-day euphoria.

I'm not here to judge anyone, I promise. I also get it: who *doesn't* want admiration and/or money? Still, if the above reasons are the *main* motivations at the forefront for writing a book, I'd consider a pause and ponder.

While I'm not a mental-health professional (I certainly advocate the important work they do) and this isn't an exhaustive listing of pros and cons, it's the benefit of my own writing and publishing experiences and represent those of many of my writing friends and clients. Apply these observations as you see fit.

Also, if you have one or two of what I deem the "often-hidden, questionable" reasons for writing, that *doesn't* in any way mean that you shouldn't write or publish your book. It's just better to stay honest with yourself and adjust expectations early in the process—your book and your own peace of mind will thank you for it.

Write It!

Talking 'bout Timelines: Gauging How Long It Takes and How Many Drafts You Need

Much consideration goes into figuring out how long you'll work on your drafts, but here are a few guiding questions and some of my experiences for insight into what to expect:

Quick considerations

- Is this your first time writing a book-length project?

- Is this the first time you've written nonfiction?

If the answer to either of these questions is yes, then expect a learning curve. Build time in for either workshopping the material or working with a freelance editor to get suggestions and personalized feedback, or (ideally) both. Taking a credit or noncredit class or getting a beta reader who offers suggestions are two other supportive ideas for first-time nonfiction authors.

Other considerations in the time equation

How many other obligations do you have at work and in your personal life? If you're working a full-time job, coaching a soccer team, and have a significant other and a group of friends you hang out with once a week, you need to figure out how many times/days a week and what specific times you will set aside for your draft. The more negotiable items you have in your schedule, the faster you'll likely write your draft (maybe you can coach next semester or cut back on your work hours or see your friends at book club every-other meeting instead of every meeting). Sometimes, very little if anything in one's schedule is negotiable (spouses/significant others, work hours/obligations, family/children/ parent-care), and that's fine—you'll just have to make a more conscious effort to nail down the exact times you'll write each week. I've had writing students who woke at 3:30 or 4 a.m. to put in an hour of writing before work three or four times a week; they still wrote their books, pages add up on that kind of schedule, even once or twice a week.

Do you have a quiet place to write? That could be your own office where you shut the door for an hour or three and the people in your life know not to step inside unless flames are jutting out of their skulls, and even then ... Or your place might be the public library. Or your place might be a coffee shop or your best friend's house. Generally, I find that the fewer people and the less public your "spot," the better and the more work gets done, but hey, we all have our own methods that work well. The important thing is that when you are in your spot people don't approach or interrupt you, you have as few distractions as possible. This means not checking your email five times (I'm terrible about this) or texts obsessively as a "reward" after each paragraph (oh, yes, I've checked emails before in-between each sentence—we've all been there). When you're in your spot, you should be in your zone, and not toggling back and forth between your phone and your writing. In your place, you write, write, write. Set a timer if it helps (I do that sometimes). Tell someone you know to be your warden—if they see you slacking, a mere look could suffice to get you back on track. Be your own warden with that timer—thou shalt not look up from thy document until thou hear the ringy-dingy. Go!

If you have the kind of job and financial stability where you can take a short break from your day job (called a sabbatical), that can be ideal for project development.

Paring back your social activities and freeing up your writing time(s) to have more frequency still often provides the easiest and least-frantic way to assemble a draft.

To give you an idea: most of my craft books take around four to six months to write a first draft (which doesn't count the weeks/months spent swapping drafts with beta readers/writing pals for feedback, editing other drafts, or working with a freelance editor for another whole-book edit and a proofread); my first book took about nine or ten months to write a rough draft as I worked out my chapter organizational and section-structuring preferences. I don't write every day at first; usually about three times a week, for an hour or hour-and-a-half each day on average. As the months go by and I get more and more into my subject matter (and more and more fortified by the thickness of my printed draft in its binder or the size of my accumulated digital file), I'll start writing two times a day (often in the morning and late at night, around my job schedule).

I run my books through at least two other drafts before submitting them to my publisher. In-between the first finished draft, I leave a few days or weeks for the project to "breathe." Then, I approach the editing stages with the draft that's really on the page, not the one I *think* I put on the page. I recommend this little grace period for the work to cool before editing on your own and/or before approaching beta readers or editors.

Since a stellar small press publishes my books, I've had the joy of working with a developmental editor, often scheduled a few months after I turn in my first "finished" draft (which to me, at that point, means "ready to be professionally edited by another editor"). Add some more time for the editor to work their magic and for me to correct/edit based on their wonderful suggestions, some copy editing, and a proofread, and you're looking at around a year to a year-and-a-half of writing and editing per book.

Often, I work on more than one manuscript at a time to speed up the cycle (and to keep things lively for my brain), but that gives you a benchmark of one author's process, from start to publication. Some authors spend two or three years just writing their drafts before seeking editorial guidance and that's perfectly normal and fine. **There's no winner method or loser method. Don't stress yourself out with comparisons or overwork yourself into a tizzy at a breakneck speed that doesn't feel compatible with your usual writing process.**

A lot of the timeline depends on your own schedule and dedication to your writing. I've known authors who've worked for almost a decade on their books, writing drafts and drafts of them, before showing them to anyone. While the latter pacing seems glacial to me and I'm way too impatient to wait that long, **I want to underscore that it's no contest—it'll take however long it takes based on a number of variables, some of which you can tweak**

to increase time lapses and some of which is just the way life surprises us and puts obstacles in our way to work around.

That said: writers who want to make more money off of their writing (if that is one of your goals) will need to write more frequently each day/week, with a more fleshed-out list of topics/outlines, and with more focus on the end product than an author who happily publishes one book every five or ten years.

If you want to make money, even a small amount, from your reference book, writing your first drafts in under a year each is imperative. Why? Remember that editing and publishing preparations (such as proofreading and layout and cover design) tack more time onto the entire process, which can stretch the actual time from starting the initial draft to holding a published book more into the realms of eighteen months to two years or longer from start to finish) and even outlining two or three books at a time and working on them for close releases (two or three books a year, such as in a series) can't hurt.

Whatever your pace: **the important thing is to keep working consistently on projects.**

That said, **keep in mind: we're writers, not machines cranking out data and output.** Even when we set up our schedules and our circumstances for a productive writing day, it's not as precise as a formula—there's some variety in how writing days/weeks/practices play out. **Don't get down on yourself when the schedule slows a bit or if you need to adjust for a glacial or disappointing writing day or week.** I have writing days where I might add two or three sentences (or just push around two or three sentences I wrote the day before) and writing days where I add 2,300 new words to a manuscript in one fell swoop. You can't predict something like that; you just show up, lean into the variety, and accept what arrives each day.

What's the difference? What did I do differently on the 2,300-word day than the three sentences push-around days? I have no idea. Some days water doesn't flow from the tap and other days it does. Keep in mind that there are some days when you'll schedule to write and you will stare at the cursor and barely write a word. **Those dud days befall us all, even writers on a schedule who write a few times a week. It happens. These frustrating non-productive days frequently pup up mid-manuscript** (at least for my writing students and me) **or right before a breakthrough day** of several hundred or even thousands of words. Just keep writing—whether that's tomorrow or today or next week that you reach a high-word-count day. The word faucet *will* start. **The important thing is to keep showing up; it's that hard and that easy.**

Try this exercise:

Write a list of two or three obstacles that might keep you away from your writing. Now, jot a list of five or six action steps you can take to get back on track or maneuver around them.

Decide and Divide: Organizing Sections or Chapters with Pizzazz and Ease for your Readers

To a large extent, you determine how readers will approach moving through your book based on how you order the material. What kind of flow do you want for your reader?

Here are a few popular methods:

1-2-3 Traditional Flow: Some reference books are meant to be read one hundred percent chronologically, so that chapter two builds on the basics from chapter one, and chapter three breaks down a concept that was covered in the previous chapter(s).

Thematic Flair: Other reference books organize according to theme. These types of books tend to have sections with titles that clue the reader to what will be covered in each thematic chunk of text.

Hello, Hybrids: The Peanut Butter-and-Jelly Blends: I've also read plenty of writing craft books that divide according to a blending of methods. Perhaps there's a list of top ten ideas with one chapter subsequently that delves into each of the ten concepts covered. Then, there is what I call "free-form" or "hybrid" organization. The book has a clear structure, but it invites the reader to dip and delve through chapters based on what they need most to read.

Natalie Goldberg's *Writing Down the Bones* and my *In a Flash!* are organized this way. Yes, the books can be read chronologically and make perfect sense. Or, readers can dip into where they want based on their wants. I often organize my books in a hybrid/blended method as I generally chunk similar chapters together and/or use section headings which clue readers into the contents of several chapters at once. This layered organizing principle helps readers decide where to begin. In the case of my books *In a Flash!* and *Poetry Power,* I was aware that many teachers of fiction, nonfiction, and poetry would use my books, and instead of assigning the whole text at once to their students, they may want to pinpoint topics to present to their students for a particular class or seminar.

More Methods: at-a-glance titles, lists, tables of contents, illustrations, and even glossaries with subjects paired with page numbers at the back all invite your readers immediately to the topics of interest to them at that moment.

Questions to consider when deciding on an organizational method:

Who is my target audience/ideal reader? What age and demographic groups do they include? Reference books for middle-schoolers and college students may include different vocabulary and more generalized knowledge than a book for readers who have practiced their craft for several years, who can handle far more in-depth details, and who don't want a review of the basics. Zeroing in on tone and content early in the writing or planning process will save you a lot of edits later.

What is my target audience's/ideal reader's primary *use* for my book? Will this book be used for classes? Instructors/teachers need speed and ease of finding topics in your book as they plan lessons. Casual hobbyists might not need as precise, at-a-glance organization.

What kind of pacing do I want my book to have? Is this a deep-dive into many facets of a topic? Or is this an introductory text with basic information to inspire neophytes and newbies? Or a text for intermediate practitioners, in which case only mild review would be necessary and the bulk of analysis of the topic should focus on middle-level and higher-level skills within the discipline. Or will this book be the first of a sequel or several follow-up books, all of which cover separate elements of the topic?

Will your book include interactive extras? Ebooks often include links to additional resources where readers can learn more information on the topic. Even an additional resource list and/or bibliography at the end of a reference book could enhance the content your book provides for readers. More on such resources in our next chapter.

On Exciting Options: Possibilities for Page Layout and Presenting Text with Panache

There are two kinds of reference books: the kinds that present the information in a straightforward narrative, such as anthologies and dictionaries, and reference books which include additional resources for reader participation that complement the book, either on the page itself, such as a sidebar, or beyond the text.

As you write your book, you'll encounter several formatting considerations and will make decisions about including or not.

First, there are the initial decisions about whether your book will have chapters or sections. Some books, like this one, have both.

Then, you'll decide whether you'll title those sections or not. I recommend yes to both to make it easier for your readers to glean thematic topics at a glance, but totally up to you—lots of books have just numerals or spaces and pictorial images like asterisks to divide information.

Most books include a table of contents that opens the book. Many reference books, particularly on writing topics, also include a brief introduction of a page or three to explore such ideas as: what inspired you to write this book, your experiences with or interest in this topic, and insight into the process of writing the book.

Sometimes, writers and/or publishers decide to use special fonts or typefaces to draw attention to key points.

Beyond these considerations, you have **many other exciting options for presenting text, including but not limited to:**

· Sidebars with facts or new information.

· Boxes which review key ideas.

· Outlines.

· Prompts.

· Arrows pointing out or offsetting key text.

· Numerical lists, such as of pros and cons to various methods or ideas.

- Comparison and contrast charts.

- Bullet points (ahem, like these for instance).

- An index of topics or themes or key words at the end of each chapter or at the very end of the book.

- Self-quizzes (such as what I included earlier in this book and one in my *Photography for Writers* book as well).

- Boldfacing key terms or ideas (I've done this often in my reference books; it's a cheap, effective, easy way for main ideas to leap off of the page).

- Suggestions for further study, such as PDF files and weblinks (these extras are especially pertinent since ebooks are so popular).

- Inclusion of drawings, illustrations, and/or photos.

What are some advantages of including any of the above thirteen special organizing principles?

Information you set off in a special way immediately alerts the reader to a series of steps. Special formatting also alerts the reader to pay attention for summarizing or advice. As readers, we are used to processing paragraphs and left-to-right aligned text, so any details that you set aside slows down a reader and condenses detail-rich prose to bare kernels that make it easier to process.

Budget will determine some of the options you choose. For instance, most drawings and illustrations are copyrighted and require fees and permissions to acquire. This can be done, but it will cost you time, energy, and often money. Photographs are a visual way to underscore main ideas and draw readers into a text, but they also drive up the cost of printing your book. If you are writing a book that will remain an e-book, this could be a moot point and add away! If you also want to publish print editions of your book, however, publishers might limit the number of photos included to keep your project from being cost-prohibitive.

You can frequently use other options to create continuity and a pattern in your manuscript. For instance, prompts are one of my favorite organizing principles. I offer writing prompts at the end of almost every chapter in all three of my *Flash Writing* series craft books. The exercises match the topic covered in each chapter and are meant to help the readers make the leap from the on-page "lecture" to their own art-making. I write exercises that a single writer can practice during a free-write, groups of authors can practice during a seminar or a class, or that even writing groups held informally at people's homes or online can do and then share among a group after a timed free-write.

You can also organize prompts as their own chapter at the end of the book, as with a fiction craft book I just pulled from my bookshelf. Or, you can space them semi-regularly throughout sections. Prompts might not be your favorite facet to dream up and share, and they don't need to be. Go with what makes the most sense for your book's style, tone, and topic.

Take heart: there are imaginative ways to get around this price problem. I kept the cost low for my craft book, *Photography for Writers,* by making a PDF file of most of the photos mentioned in my chapters that I then published on a special tab on my website. I provided the URL link with a note in the opening pages of my book for interested readers to check out. This decision also made perfect sense from a business and professional standpoint; readers who check out the photographic PDF often also click on my bio, my classes and books page, or my blog while there. Expensive printing problems creatively avoided! Those curious about the photos mentioned in the book can still peruse them with a lower-priced book for them and with only the cost of the website maintenance each year for me. Win-win.

Consider how each page will look and how you want readers to navigate the main ideas you present. I remember being a graduate student studying poetry, and it blew my mind when one of my favorite professors took one of my poems that was almost margin-to-margin crammed with words and started to cross out unnecessary descriptors. The resulting poem was sleeker, more to the point, and explicated the importance of white space between words and also in margins and between stanzas. Epiphany time!

Designers and magazine staff who do layout have long exploited the way they present text on a page to their great advantage, but to me it was a revelation that I've carried with me for years and share with students. Like sentence variety and integrating some incomplete sentences for emphasis and stylistic considerations, **including white space around some text carries the potential for highlighting or emphasizing ideas without getting too repetitious or heavy-handed.**

As you write your reference book, it will be up to you and, later and in some cases, up to your editor or layout designer or publisher's input as well, to decide how much white space and special formatting make sense for the way you've structured your book. **There's no magic formula and every writer or publishing professional will have slightly different preferences as far as ordering and/or allowing space in layout.**

A lot of page layout and organization of information is based on personal preferences and your own learning style. How do *you* process new information? Ask a few friends which of the listed organizing principals would appeal most to them.

You can also give this exercise a spin that I recommended to a client. Take a page or a chapter from your book and organize it in three different ways. For instance, use an outline or bullet points in part of one chapter. Then, organize the same passage in boxes or sidebars. Lastly, shake it up one more time and try boldfacing a few key ideas. Print out your three samples and compare/contrast. Ask a few friends for second opinions of the most-appealing method to read.

Good news, organizing a reference book is not an all-or-nothing proposition. Many authors, including yours truly, have used several of these methods concurrently and then omitted others that aren't their style (for me, an index isn't my jam, so I don't include one in my books).

Try this exercise:

Pull three or four craft books from your shelf or load them on your e-reader. Make some notes on any of the thirteen organizing methods I've listed and how you, as a reader, react to encountering them. Do any annoy you or slow you down through the text? Do any of them make it easier to navigate the chapter or section?

Bonus exercise: type or photocopy the list of thirteen elements on this page and keep it handy as you write your chapters. After each initial draft, consult the list and add one of the organizing elements to your chapter in your second draft.

Me-ouch! The Not-So-Small Matter of Tone

You haven't lived until you've had a rejection-slip delivery on your birthday. Yep, totally happened to me yesterday afternoon.

First, I shrugged my shoulders. Then, I noted the rejection in my writing notebook (yes, I keep a tactile one in addition to using Submittable online) and thought, "I'm sorry that you've rejected three of my favorite poems. Now somebody else will get to publish them."

Okay, truthfully, that's a lot more self-assured and bravado-filled than it felt in my head or in my gut. Even though I'm sure the editors had no idea it was my birthday (why would they?), getting a chilly rejection slip *still* pinched and was sucky timing.

But it's also worth noting that the rejection in no way ruined a day otherwise filled with a boatload of acceptance: calls and messages of cheer from friends and clients, a delicious coconut cake, and a zippy Zoom with my birthday-twin niece who had just gotten (I am not kidding) a giant white plush-tiger toy whose face is bigger than hers and which she could barely hold up to the camera. Happy sixth, darling girl, and happy significantly more than six a few times to me!

As I described my birthday-timed rejection to a fabulous writing friend today, I slung in a little one-word encapsulation that I knew would set the tone of this experience: "Me-ouch!"

I then described for my talented pal how sometimes, when I say it aloud, I make a little cat paw with dagger claws with my right hand to add an additional flourish of friskiness to an otherwise bummer of a situation. A little prolonged gusto on the "-ouch" part never hurt to set a mood, either. We both had a chuckle as I suggested liberal sprinkling of my sassy conjugation far and wide.

As a word hybrid, part of its charm is its fanciful spelling (the word nerd and grammarian in me really did just pause and think, 'Hmm ... Should I transcribe that as -u in the middle as in 'ouch' or to complete the –ow of 'meow?'" You may commence laughing now).

"Me-ouch!" immediately clued my friend into how I approached the heavy topic of rejection as well as orienting her as a reader within the text—yeah, it was a downer topic but it would be handled in a warm, comedic way that would make neither of us feel bogged down by the reality. **In writing our craft books, we can apply the same attention to diction choices to create a tone that is uniquely part of our own prose style.**

There's a reputation in nonfiction for stuffiness. After all, we're talking about real-life stuff, "facts" and figures and concrete examples and explications here! We have established our credibility as well as why we are *the* writer to write this book, and we don't want to compromise that, right?

Well, not so fast ...

There are as many approaches to tone in nonfiction reference books as there are in any other type of writing, from poetry and fiction to memoir and graphic novels. I remember reading Gayle Brandeis' *Fruitflesh: Seeds of Inspiration for Women Who Write* (and choosing it as a text for a subsequent online class I taught) and finding her sensuous, lyric language refreshing and inspiring. Students responded very well to her thematic word choices that brought each chapter to vivid life. Another delightful writing text that forever altered my view on what's possible for making a craft book lively and energetic is Sage Cohen's *Writing the Life Poetic: An Invitation to Read and Write Poetry*. Both texts are packed with knowledge, passion, and specific imagery that not only invites but beckons readers to take this journey with them.

Now, I don't know about you, but **that's always my aim for my writing: for my personality to come across in my prose or verse.** Yeah, there are plenty of times when seriousness and just-the-facts are the way to go (car accidents and funerals spring to mind— sorry for *these* massive bummers!), but **I don't believe a craft book should be restricted to rigid formulas or dry, stuffy diction choices.** Just ... *non, nein, nyet,* and please no!

A little focus on your tone can keep readers turning pages to follow whatever points you want them to explore—they'll be so entertained that it won't seem like time (or pages) are ticking by at all. **We should want to deliver key information in such a way, often anecdotally or within context, that we embed compelling storytelling into the structure of our books.**

My biggest tip for authors working on tone is to consider your target audience for your book. Even if (perhaps especially when) you're just beginning to pen your book. Don't overthink this; just roll with your gut instincts. Some writers secretly pick somebody they know in real life and address their book to that person—use whatever works to get the words flowing in a focused, fun way. If you don't know a person you'd consider your ideal reader, no sweat. Jot a few (say: five or six) qualities you want your ideal reader to possess. Keep this list with you as you write.

My ideal reader list for this book is: clever, intuitive, ambitious, curious, hopeful, and precise. If I had to list a few additional qualities for my target market, I'd pick humorous, educated, open-hearted, and insightful.

It also doesn't matter if some of the qualities you list are paradoxes (you probably spot one or two in my list above). There's room for more than one tone within a reference book; in fact, depending on the theme(s) or chapter focus, more than one tone can enrich complex subjects and keep material from reading as either too heavy-handed or too flip. Mixing and matching, as with a delectable à la carte meal, can be surprisingly delicious. Just watch how many combinations you pour back-to-back—variety is a tasty spice in measure but barfy if mixed in willy-nilly and with no thought to how the ingredients mesh or don't.

A few things to consider as you write (and later, edit) your work for tone

- If you had to pick three words to describe your nonfiction tone, what would they be? Mine are *playful, informed*, and *connective*. If I had another word, I'd pick either *expansive* or *big-picture*.

- What's one quality you *never* want in your tone? Mine is *condescension*.

- How often does your chapter/section switch tones? Are there any instances where the tone shift feels unnatural? If so, look for specific sentences and even individual words that cause the uncomfortable shift and replace them.

- Do you ever use hybrid or slang terms? Do you use too many of these? Or sometimes too few?

- Are there any places where tone overshadows content? That is, are there places where the prose is decorative and draws attention away from meaning or themes which should be the primary purpose in our writing? Tone should enhance content (think of content as the main event), and not the other way around.

Into each of our lives a little "Me-ouch" must fall. As we write our reference books, let's keep the door propped open for diction choices that underscore not only our target audience and a welcoming tone but also support the content of our books.

A Small Step Sideways: Sustaining Your Project through the Unexpected

The bad-news bomb arrived, as such things tend to, on an upbeat day when I'd finally cleared my schedule for the afternoon to write another chapter in this book. (Incidentally, another popular way to receive this snarky soul-sucker is via text, but I digress.)

All week, I'd made promising plans to open a word processing file first-thing and get cracking. I managed to suppress the urge to peek inside my inbox before writing … for about twenty seconds. Yep, you read that correctly. Seconds.

Now, I'm no lightweight—give me a project and a vision and I'll get that thing popping by deadline, if not before. So, believe me when I say, I'm still very much a sucker for my own methods of diversion and delusion. What could be the harm in just one little peruse? You know, in case a client had an emergency question about a manuscript I was editing or there was a deal on widgets and furbelows I just had to have [wink-wink].

We tell ourselves such lies, and the temptation to scroll through new messages is no stranger to this writing life. We all sometimes begin what could be a perfectly-open road to getting those words on the page by sabotaging our own efforts in deceptively simple ways from the get-go. Be it "quickly" cleaning the veggie crisper of its green goop that's been sliming for who knows how many days, walking the dog "for just a few blocks," streaming "just a couple minutes" of this episode, etc. For some reason, at least for me, it's either email or leftover, lagging chores that suddenly seem like a four-alarm fire when I should be fulfilling my promise to myself to write.

Needless to say, one look at the sender's name in my box—an acquaintance I hadn't heard from in months—turned a little joy key inside of me, like winding a jewelry box with a spinning ballerina atop the lid. I was already anticipating good news. Eagerly, I shoved aside opening my writing file and getting started. *I'll just quickly see what they've been up to lately.*

Well, it started well—both my intentions to write *and* the first three newsy, upbeat paragraphs of the email. I was smiling. I was even chortling at one point at a witty reference. I genuinely liked this friend's company and was eager for more connection. The rest, however, was a speedy decline—a quick bad-news bomb in "reveal-and-run" mode, combined with asking for a favor, and then slapdash well wishes tacked on as if the bomb-and-ask hadn't just happened.

Ick.

Well, there's the real reason for getting in touch, I thought, heart in my heels, knowing I'd just side-swiped myself.

You guessed it, this is the only chapter in this book about writing that's not about writing. Or, at least, it's about *not* writing. Say *what*?!

Being on the receiving end of bad news is exceedingly disruptive, especially for creative pursuits. It's especially disorienting when the bad news comes out of left field.

Yeah, people can make meaningful art from their pain and it's a fabulous way to process complex emotions (like I'm doing now), but the caveat (at least for me and many of my writing students) is that **some time usually needs to pass between the receiving of the rupture and the processing of it to make art that makes sense and doesn't seek to throw the other person under the bus** and then drive back over them.

The day you get the call that a loved one has been diagnosed or a friend's marriage is on the rocks or the vet says your beloved feline isn't doing well is *not* the same day you're going to sit down merrily with your draft. Oh, you might jot some thoughts or type out a diatribe of whys to clear your brain (all very healthy in the short-run) but when you receive some really hard-to-swallow bitter pills that are life's biggies (incidentally: life's "smallies," like this message from my acquaintance, ain't no peach, either), it's not the day for clear, organized prose. It's just hard enough to keep it together and not let frustration, sorrow, tears, or anger mar everything, let alone to maintain rational, clear prose.

I repeat: **don't attempt to write your project on the same day you receive disappointing or hard news, as if nothing much is up. Self-care is crucial for writers. Big projects require a lot of focus, and when we're still reeling from hurt it's nearly impossible to add immediate depth and value to what we've written.**

Take a break. You're not going to write resonant prose when you're barely holding on. Be compassionate about your emotions. Sit in them for a while. These are honest, authentic responses to the blow you just sustained.

After I read the email, and then read it a second and third time, I knew in my gut that my creative writing day was over. No use. My thoughts were a jumbled glob. Yes, I did plenty of other things that day—including a walk, paying some bills—life can't just halt because of upsetting news. But as for my writing, I knew it would be better to take a short hiatus and get at it another day, which I did.

Here's the challenging part of all of this: some life circumstances are sustained storms. If you're going through a very long, arduous life change that involves multiple months or years, such as child custody or being sued or job hunting, at some point in the process, you will need to keep writing to continue your project or else you'll stall out completely. For such circumstances, be gentle with yourself. **If all you can write each week is a paragraph or two, it's all progress. Do what you can and increase how much more you write whenever you can. A simple formula, although not always easy to measure each time. Be flexible with yourself and your muse.**

Only you can gauge whether a few hours away or a few days' break would be better. The important thing is to give yourself a small break to process and then head back to your work. Horrible things happen to everyone, writers included. They might tip you over for a bit, but in the end, your determination will keep you heading back to continue what you started.

Also, here's the thing: nothing breaks us open and brings out new ideas more than sudden unwelcomed vulnerability. It probably looks weird to see it (it feels kind of odd to type it, too), but **don't let this opportunity go untapped**. Sometimes, our personal struggles lead us to important discoveries for topics to include in our books. That's one of the silver linings of a chapter like this.

Now, I'm *not* suggesting you make your book a dumping ground for your own angst, but **to communicate with authenticity there's lots of room to expand your book when your own experiences and even questions inform it. Don't shy away from going to some hard places once you feel collected and focused enough to do so.** Before then, don't overly rush it.

If you wonder or struggle with something, a reader will, too, and will be interested that you brought the topic into the book. **Readers will connect with your sensitivity and bravery, even if you never fully dish the dirty details on how the situation hurt you most**—you don't need to share every detail. That's your personal beeswax, after all. Readers have inherent truth-detectors based on word choices and so many other elements of how you write—provide a sketch with a few pertinent details, and they'll quite aptly fill in the rest.

Just keep writing. Except, of course, when you need to take a breather to gather your molecules together into some semblance of order before you gather the words; that's perfectly fine, too.

Diamond with a Flaw or Pebble Without: Seven Tips for Knowing When Your Book Draft is Done

Ah, the ubiquitous ending! Look, endings are hard and angst-riddled for everyone, from the end of a vacation or job to the goodbye of a relationship or a friendship or, yes, even the finale of a draft.

What are some ways we know that it's time to put up the bye-bye banners and start planning for our next projects?

You've printed out a copy. Long manuscripts can read very differently when you hold them in your hands like a published book rather than when scrolling endlessly on a screen. I recommend this to all of my clients. Double-side print to save trees, but please do take the effort and the ink, at least once. It's tremendously helpful and an indicator of where there might yet be holes in the manuscript.

You've let it rest for a few days (or weeks) to read it anew, chapter by chapter, beginning to end. I'm never one hundred percent certain on the day that I write the "last" words that it's really the last thing I'll add to my draft. Usually, it's not. After I perceive a near-conclusion, I let the draft breathe and work on something else for a while, returning later to reread the passage and see if there's anything I'd like to add, move around, or edit.

You've gotten a first (and maybe a second) opinion. This is where it can be super handy to have a trusted beta reader (or hire one), a fellow writer to swap pages with, or a pal who likes to read and who will note if they think there's anything awkward or that needs to be explicated further, especially to latter parts of the book when the writing can get slow and tiring. Ask this kind reader if they feel like there's any topic missing and if the current ending reads smoothly and satisfyingly.

You've achieved "best possible order" of all chapters/material. Just because you wrote certain paragraphs, chapters, or sections in one order over the weeks and months doesn't mean that you can't move pieces/chapters. Feel free to move some passages into different chapters; I do that all of the time.

You've made a list and covered all of the topics, staying open throughout the whole process to add to it. When you jotted notes or made outlines and plans for your book, you most likely didn't have every single idea prepared before writing the first paragraph. Give yourself permission not only to gather new ideas along the way but even once you're pretty sure you're writing the last chapter.

You've edited … a few times. Nobody's first draft is their best draft. I repeat: *nobody's* first draft is their best draft. I run my books through three edits (at least) myself before working with developmental and content editors—so that's five edits. As you edit, look for errors: spelling or grammatical errors, errors of logic, unintended repetitions (like mice, those little beasties tend to multiply), and the like. Since you're writing nonfiction, you must fact-check as well.

When you know, you know. You have an innate sense of completion. Or the dreadful opposite, a missing wheel. Okay, granted many writers are perfectionists and some of us have been known to fuss with one paragraph for weeks or longer. So this one might not apply to you, especially if this is your first book, but still … Books have symmetry and shape—when our writing isn't flowing or something seems out of shape, there's often a dissatisfied feeling that lingers.

A word of caution, though: if you know that you're a perfectionist or going through a period where you feel insecure about your writing, make sure to get a second opinion before tearing apart your manuscript into pieces again—you likely won't need to. As Voltaire and others have said: "Perfect is the enemy of good." No need to strive for absolute perfection.

All readers ask for is a highly readable yet ever-so-slightly-flawed book (all books, by the way, are). I still find random typos and missing words within big-name, traditionally-published books as I'm reading—and it never makes me think less of the author or the editors. Look, despite all efforts, now and again an error sneaks through, even after several people have carefully combed a manuscript. Don't beat yourself up over it. That said, still comb through your manuscript and get others to do so. I've also read books *riddled* with errors and that *does* reflect poorly and denote carelessness to readers, which is not the impression you want to give readers.

Which leads us to this little wisdom nugget from Confucius: "Better a diamond with a flaw than a pebble without." Some flaws will get through no matter how much editing or second- or third-looking we do, but in the end nit-picking or being highly self-critical will do as much (if not more) harm than thinking our initial draft is perfect straight out of our brains and with no editing. Seek a midway approach, and your book will be much better for it.

Then, the hardest part: practice the art of knowing you've done all that you can, writing this project with all your passion and abilities. Deep breath. And let it go.

Building Your
Writing Career:
Editing, Pre-Publication,
and Marketing

Not Going it Alone, Part One: on Writing-Swap Partners

As I write this chapter, it's a Sunday afternoon in November. In typical rural East Coast US fashion, the sky holds a subdued, somber gray. Have you seen painter Andrew Wyeth's landscapes? It's *that* hue of autumnal sky: sullen, flat, beautifully spare light that is pearlescent and satin-y at the same time. It's the kind of weather that inspires yawns and slow-paced movement and intellectual activity rather than walks with the family dog or drives through winding roads for the pleasure of covering miles.

Time to turn inward.

With the chill wind picking up, tumbling-down brown leaves, and the potential of rain or snowflakes at any moment (this morning I spotted a few outside the window), it's the perfect day for introverted pursuits—to curl up with a novel, work on a project, or stream a movie and zone out (in the sense of "in the zone," not mindlessness).

The thing about writing is that it's also most often a solitary activity. Even authors studying in university creative writing programs or writers who teach *still* spend most our writing lives alone at our desks with the muse. While the necessity to turn inward and block out the outside distractions will remain a part of the writing process, I heavily encourage my writing students and clients (and my introverted self) to reach out and keep connecting with my fellow writers—if not in the drafting stage, then definitely in the editing stages.

So what's so great about getting feedback, anyway? I believe in the power of feedback. Now, not just any willy-nilly feedback, but informed suggestions and support from another author. Critiques help writers spot out our own blind spots. You know, those areas we think we've added to a manuscript, but we haven't, or passages that are confusing or vague. What haven't we included in a chapter or a section that we should? What repetitions occur that we could omit? What passages are awkward or could use more details or specific examples?

Then, there's the camaraderie aspect of interacting with fellow writers. It's fun to "talk shop" about how hard and yet satisfying it is to write a book. Yeah, complaining to your spouse or sibling or best friend can let off steam, but there's a particular level of support and been-there-felt-that which only a fellow author can deliver. Plus, having a first or second reader to ask some niggling questions about the writing can be very reassuring.

Okay, so getting another writer's opinion can be handy, but where in the world do we go to find such a person? I hear you; many writers, especially those just starting out, don't yet know a bunch of authors and editors. I vividly recall being there.

Some of the top places to get feedback that I suggest to my clients and students are:

Take an online creative writing class. Ask among students who share your interests if anyone would be interested in swapping manuscripts to offer each other feedback. Also, even if no one in the class strikes you as particularly into your style of writing, you can always **ask your creative writing teacher if they know of anyone** who offers beta reads, swaps in kind (where both writers give feedback), or editorial guidance. Creative writing teachers are well-informed and often generously direct students to websites or connect students to fellow writers via text or email who may be interested in workshopping. The thing is, though, you have to take the initiative to ask. Even if the teacher doesn't offer you an immediate recommendation, just having your request on their radar may lead to recommendations later—it's always worth asking and planting the seed of the idea! Authors often fear they'll mismatch with a writing partner, whether someone whose suggestions are out of left field and make little sense or someone who takes feedback but is stingy or vague in return—hey, like every other relationship and friendship, it can happen (sure, it's happened to me, too) or it can surprise you and evolve nicely over time (yep, luckily it's happened to me, too). No guarantees—but when are there ever?

Begin with cautiously optimistic, basic expectations and as much let's-try-this attitude as possible with a one-time trade and see where it goes from there. If you begin a swap and, after trading work once or twice, find that you're not meshing with the author's draft (say it's more violent or sexual or vague or slapstick than the prose you read or write), it's perfectly acceptable either to write the other author that you'd really like to offer feedback but that you think your skillset won't be able to give them what their manuscript could most benefit from at this time **or** to say that you don't have time for a while to swap work again. The latter of which is true, after all. None of us has time for work that we know makes us uncomfortable or unsure; we could better spend that time on our own work.

There can be a bit of trial and error in finding a solid fit, but don't give up easily.

Remember that creative writing teachers and book club leaders are often excellent advocates and literary matchmakers, so to speak, who probably know a bunch more creative folks who'd enjoy sharing work than just one person. One work partner might be a horror while the other quickly becomes a trusted friend. You just never know—there's a good amount of serendipity and timing involved.

Ask that friend of yours who is super into reading (perhaps from your book club). Even if they aren't writers, readers notice symbolism, story structure, characterization, and dialogue, among many other elements of writing. Even if they don't have an MFA or MA, avid readers can pinpoint spots where the writing goes off-track or gets repetitious or where they'd like additional details.

Join a free writing site online—Facebook has a bunch of private writing groups for just about any genre you can think of. Once you've introduced yourself and proven yourself an interested member by posting for a few days, make a quick post asking if anyone is interested in either offering feedback or if they know of a skilled beta reader or editor who may be interested in offering quality feedback.

Go to a reading at your local community's coffee shop or university/college. Many coffee shops and schools host a once-monthly reading or quarterly open-mic activities where like-minded literary folks can mingle before or afterward. What better way to make a new writing friend?

There are now many excellent online readings sponsored by literary magazines. Who doesn't like sincere praise? Getting a complimentary text or email or message stating that you appreciated their work excites those invited to read at these events. As with making any new friend, don't lead with asking to swap work right away. Mention that you're also a writer and would love to "talk shop" anytime. If more emails or texts arrive in response, then broach the subject by offering to share work sometime, for feedback in kind, if that should be of interest. Approach gently but optimistically.

Join a creative writing group or form your own. Writers tend to love hanging out with other writers. Why? Because we understand this writing path—its challenges and thrills—in a way others likely don't. Realize that fellow writers might not lead with the idea of swapping work or offering each other suggestions, but that in a writing group that meets, say monthly, you'll receive a bunch of different opinions on your work at once and there's likely one or two fellow writers whose suggestions resonate the most. These will be the folks whom you politely inquire, whether verbally or through a short text or email outside of group, if they'd be interested in offering feedback on more pages/ longer work.

Don't bombard this kind person all at once, but you could certainly get feedback on additional chapters this way, working through large chunks or sections of a whole book over a few months' time. One of my most motivated swap buddies and I have done this and have provided constructive feedback and suggestions on many chapters from our nonfiction. This process keeps us both encouraged in our latest projects, especially in the murky middles which can be tough in any long project. Be a considerate and attentive trading buddy. Now and again, treat this friend to an extra critique or beverage of their choice or other thoughtful token (a book by their favorite author, say) to show them that their time and advice are invaluable to you.

Make a check-in chum. Here's a fun alternative: what if you're running short on time but still could use an uplift? Another awesome writing pal and I set up what we call Sunday Check-in. For the past several months, instead of trading pages we trade a paragraph or two to email about what we wrote the past week. It's excellent accountability. Sometimes, we describe a word count or the chapter in our novels. Other times, we detail the editing process or having a breakthrough/breakdown with a character. Whatever we've done that week, we describe it to the other and then ask the other author about her work. It's just as motivating and magical as a swap. Sometimes, we trade comical memes about writing or writing quotes that resonate, but there's always cheer and camaraderie that make me look forward to each check-in.

How to ask for specific feedback

The first time or two you swap writing it can be helpful to both writers to note if there are any areas in particular that you want them to look for, such as: "I'm worried that chapter two needs more examples. Do you like the examples I have? Or would others be clearer?" It can also be useful to reference a certain page or paragraph in your note.

When I swap book chapters and other writing with one of my swap partners, about fifty percent of the time (or more) I include a little paragraph referencing two or three passages I'm wondering about and ask for their specific feedback on those areas. I also always note that I'm open to other feedback, should the partner want to give more feedback, but I realize that they are all very busy folks with much on their plates and I don't want to overload them.

In return, I offer that my partners can send their own questions with their chapters if they wish.

Three top tips for critique-partner etiquette

1. Pay attention to the other person's schedule as well as your own.

Look ahead a week or even a month at a time. Realize that some weeks or months the person might not be able to offer

additional feedback or that you won't—or that you'll need to extend your deadline to give quality feedback. Set up a loose schedule (say: "Swap Saturdays, where we'll send each other ten pages or a chapter and give feedback by a week later") and be flexible and generous with your scheduling and also prepared to let your buddy off the hook sometimes if they need more space and time for the moment or indefinitely.

One new swap partner and I traded work earlier this year and had an insightful trade going for three or four swaps, but then his schedule made swapping too much for his daily responsibilities, and I could tell that it was not easy news to share that he felt burned out. I stepped back, offering an open door if he'd like to swap in the future.

It can also be helpful, before sending your writing attachment, especially if you haven't heard from a writing pal for a while, to send a quick text or email to double-check if your friend still has time to read your work: "We still set to swap chapters on Thursday this week?"

Look, life happens to all of us; pay attention to your swap partners' needs as well as to your own, and graciously offer to reschedule or put a pause on trading work if one or both of you become overwhelmed or run long on unexpected activities, such as during holidays. Another writing partner and I used to trade in November (final exam month!) each year, but since we both taught, he and I moved it to October—a less-stressful month for both of our schedules, and we've had a longstanding swap for that month ever since.

2. If you suggest or take a trade, by all means be responsible.

If you're going to run late for any reason in delivering feedback, send a text or email with an estimate of when you will reply and then make that new deadline, no ifs, ands, or buts. There's nothing more disappointing than a person who greedily takes suggestions on their own writing and then makes empty promises about the other person's work, never offering any feedback at all or putting far less effort and detail into their feedback. Make sure you pull your own weight. **Set the bar high, and only accept trades from others who will hold you to it or move on. If you receive spotty feedback or perpetual excuses from a swap partner, dust off your feet and move on quickly to someone who will love getting your work and giving you feedback in return.**

3. If you receive suggestions from a critique partner, always send a follow-up thank you text or message for their time, even if you don't like their feedback and don't plan to ask for their advice again.

While it is your prerogative not to continue getting suggestions if you're not satisfied—you need feedback that offers relevant suggestions, after all—it still pays to be gracious.

The literary world is a small one and word gets around. Be nicer than you think you need to be, even if disappointed sometimes. It's normal to encounter some suggestions that are confusing, off-theme, or just don't work for our goals, but just as often, we'll get valuable suggestions that help us to add depth, details, and focus to our work. Yes, be considerate about all feedback, but also know that it's ultimately your decision which advice meets your goals for your writing.

Not Going it Alone, Part Two: on Beta Readers

Last chapter, I noted some reasons why getting a second or third opinion enhances our writing. I also noted some ways and places to find a writing-swap partner. We explored the free option of an individual trade of manuscript pages, often a chapter at a time but in any agreed-upon quantity partners prefer, as well as checking in weekly with a writing pal.

Another excellent way to get feedback is to find a beta reader.

What's the difference between a beta reader and a manuscript-swap partner, anyway? There's some wiggle room here, but the short answer is that beta readers tend to give a larger overview of the material. They may or may not be editors or fellow craft-practitioners, such as writers in a writing class.

Beta readers highlight some of the same issues editors do—such as plot, chapter structure, pacing, problems with vague examples, and the like—but they *don't* comb through your manuscript giving copious suggestions line-by-line or comment paragraph by paragraph as editors, they *don't* often make grammar suggestions, and sometimes they *don't* offer suggestions or other resources for continued research of your topic as editors or swap partners might well do.

For both types of readers (beta readers and manuscript-swap partners), expect that they will read all of your work and offer specific feedback.

Beta readers come in both the paid and unpaid varieties. I've known many students who found a beta reader within one of my classes and other students who found a beta reader online at a literary reading or in a social-media group for writers—all great places to make literary friends who might be willing to beta for you in exchange for your reading and writing expertise on their work of art in-progress. Betas tend to look big-picture in their feedback, which is invaluable for early drafts when nitpicking editing would bog down a writer.

If you've ever participated in NaNoWriMo, the November novel-writing challenge each year (a wonderful challenge I've taken part in and recommend), that's another excellent place to network for an interested beta reader. Check out their website for more information about the challenge and networking opportunities. There are forums and groups that form each year during the challenge which could lead to extended communication if two particular writers click and wish to beta for each other. One or two of my students have mentioned finding their beta reader in a forum during the challenge and then continuing to beta after November. Worth a shot.

There are also beta readers for hire. **If you know other writers, say from an online group or class or writing circle, ask if they or anyone they know offers beta reads. Also ask if they know a skilled freelance editor—can't hurt to get as much info and as many resources in your book's corner as possible.**

Why? Here's the thing: I get most of my editing clients through word-of-mouth recommendations from satisfied clients. I *don't* list beta reading on my personal website, though. Why not? Developmental editing and other literary and teaching projects are my top priority, but when the opportunity to offer beta reading letters of three or four pages of feedback show up in my inbox as a query and I can tell by the writing sample that the author is articulate and has thought through their book and has something special, you better believe I take the gig if I have time.

Many editors I know also don't necessarily list beta reading or generalized feedback on their websites, either, but if you prepare your materials and present yourself as focused and articulate, they often become interested in the gig. My advice: prepare a sample of either five or ten pages or the first chapter, your contact information, as well as a one-paragraph synopsis of your project (pretend you're writing the back cover of your book for the reader—then send that focused paragraph describing your book in an email to the perspective reader) and le voila! Depending on their schedules, they may likely contact you at least to discuss your project at greater length or to recommend a colleague of theirs who might offer the same service. Always worth a shot.

You could also do a website search for a beta reader. Include such keywords as "beta readers" or "editorial feedback" or the like. Also, include your genre, in this case, "nonfiction" and any other subject-matter words related to your theme. I once found a beta reader for a Regency fiction project this way online. She was a member of a large, professional writing organization I belonged to for two years, and her name was listed on a database of respected betas. She was just starting out and worked at very reasonable rates in return for me writing a good review once I was a satisfied customer. Done and done!

The art of the cold-ask

If you cold-ask a professional for a beta read (that is: you don't know this writer

personally and have never spoken to them on either social media or via text/email) approach it as seriously and carefully as you would submitting your work to a literary magazine or agent.

Remember that you are asking a fellow writer to give up time on their own projects to invest in yours—this is a lot to ask of anyone, whether paid or (especially) unpaid. Make sure always to include details about your project (in synopsis form is ideal), a word count of your project, and ask politely about their rates and scheduling opportunities. You can either go ahead and send sample work from the project with your query or offer to send an excerpt at their convenience (make sure to have this excerpt ready *before* emailing the freelancer to give the best impression when/if they ask for it).

Here's some insight from the other side of the publishing desk that I hope can offer insight: **it is amazing to me how many beta and editing queries I get where the author tells me just the title or genre of their book and the word count and literally *nothing* else about their project. I want to be wowed and to feel the author's enthusiasm flying off of the screen—potential clients who show me zest and focus grab my attention and I usually have a blast working with them because I believe in their work.**

A single-sentence cold query with a word count and title doesn't excite me at all to invest weeks in someone else's project. The majority of ill-prepared potential clients disappear once I ask for the materials I've listed here so I can make a more-informed decision about their work. This is also a way to winnow away potential clients who either aren't quite ready for professional feedback or who are lazy about stepping up to bat with their book's details.

I certainly don't expect perfection or even paragraphs upon paragraphs about a fellow writer's project, but **I always aim to work with fellow writers who can make the most of what they've written and who are ready to do the work. Show that you are ready and invested in your project's success. Proofread your description once or twice, and then get a friend to proof it before sending it.**

By the way, it's perfectly fine to ask about potential rates (I never mind that at all), but don't lead with that question. Introduce yourself and your work first. You could also include how long you've been writing, any literary magazine publications you've had (if you have any, no worries if you don't), any other investments such as writing conferences or writing programs/classes/workshops, and how you learned of this editor. (If you read their book or publication online or their website, include that detail.)

Potential clients who care enough to tell me at least what they've invested in their writing and how they learned about me always stand a much better shot of my taking on their projects than the one- or two-sentence askers.

So, while you *can't* just expect that all editors are open to beta reading, you certainly could query an editor and see if they are open to perusing your project (even better if you drop the name of the person/client who recommended them and/or your teacher's name to show your dedication to your craft). You never know.

Professionals are often eager to work with up-and-coming authors and passionate about working on projects that show potential. Make sure you peruse their website to get a feeling for what projects they've published or worked on with other authors recently, and then feel free to mention any projects they've done that interest you or relate to your work. I've named-dropped projects when I've hired professionals for some projects, and it's perfectly acceptable and shows that you've done your research.

Many beta readers are open to questions or notes about what areas you'd like particular feedback on, too, but don't presume it—can't hurt to check, going in.

Yeah, but what if it's a giant no or complete silence?

That said: don't blame yourself or your writing if it's *a no, thank you*. Reply back to the editor, thanking them for their time, and ask if they know of any beta readers who might be interested. A writing student of mine found her beta reader this way, and they worked on multiple projects together happily. Just last week, I had a request for a project that I really like but just don't have time to take on until six months from now, which I understand might be too long to wait, depending on the author's timeline for the project. I offered the writer the opportunity of working with me in six months or, in case they'd rather not wait, details of an excellent editor friend of mine in the meantime.

Another possibility is that you'll invest effort in introducing yourself to this professional and literally never hear back a peep. Ugh. I'm sorry about that, and I always aim to reply at least with *no thanks* to queries, but the truth is that sometimes editors won't get back to you at all. Consider that a no and move on. Emails add up and get lost or forgotten in folders, and many freelancers swamped with projects stop taking clients for months or even years until they catch up. It's super unfair and frustrating, but it happens.

If you do happen to hear back and it's a no, I understand that it stings (I've heard deafening silence and also had the no when trying to hire betas and editors—so I feel your pain). **Whatever you do, though, refrain from sending a diatribe or a gut-reaction response.** It's totally understandable to want to do so, but also bad form to send it. Call up a writing friend and vent, instead, to get it out. As I noted earlier in the book, the literary and publishing community is quite small and connected, so the last thing you want to do is send a negative experience out into the world that could rare up to bite you with the next editor. (Yes, editors really do talk shop a lot, and you don't want that knee-jerk email or text following your name around like a stench.)

Like creative writing teachers, editors have a bevy of talented professionals within their network that may just include the perfect beta reader for your project. Always thank any editor who goes out of their way to offer a personal response, web links, or a contact's information (many get multiple dozens of queries a year and it's not personal—they just don't have the time to reply to everyone, much as it gut-wrenches writers). Betas and editors who share any kind of information or contacts with writers demonstrate a level of generosity that is above and beyond professional courtesy.

We remember writers who show appreciation for any tidbit of information shared favorably. Should you ever email in the future for another project, you never know, they *might just* have time to work with you the next time. **Build bridges with contacts now, even if you're not reaping the rewards yet of working with them.**

The bottom line about working with betas or swap partners

Working with beta readers or manuscript-swap partners is a case of you get out of it what you put into it. Send what you think is your best writing; if it's not something you're proud of yet, keep working on it before sending. If the material you send is last–minute and slapdash or unrelated to most of the manuscript or you don't include a question or aspect you'd like the reader to look for or, conversely, you aren't open to feedback that wasn't on your list, then you're wasting valuable opportunities to sharpen and expand your work.

Stay as open as possible as you read and sort through suggestions from others. Sometimes, suggestions that at first seem out of left field end up being helpful when trying them later.

It can take some trial and error to find a pal to swap work with or a beta reader or three.

Stay open to getting multiple sets of feedback. Some months I swap work with three or four fellow authors I've known for years—some from creative writing classes and some from teaching and publishing—and glean helpful feedback in differing ways from each author and truly enjoy reading their latest work. But much like friendships and love partnerships, keep persevering and once you do develop a rapport with a fellow writer, their support is priceless to the writing and/or editing processes. Plus, many beta readers or swap partners are then available for future projects—win-win.

Whether you get free feedback from a fellow writer and return the favor in kind by giving advice back or paying a freelancer for their time, **getting an outside opinion can save much time and frustration in the long run. Especially before submitting later drafts to a publisher or agent or before self-publishing. I recommend getting at least one—if not more—sets of eyes on your manuscript.**

It's *always* still your book, but getting direct feedback from at least one or two readers before going after a larger readership will ensure a smoother, more fulfilling read in the long run and helps the author to grow as a writer. I'm working on my seventh book that will be published, and I eagerly still seek the opinion of swap partners and have hired beta readers before. **Attention to craft is invaluable at every stage of our writing careers.**

To Agent or Not to Agent

Whenever you write a manuscript and want to traditionally publish it, you have two basic options: you can seek agent representation to submit for you or you can submit your writing on your own. Below are some tips that illustrate some pros and cons to both options. Keep in mind that it's just one writer's POV. Weigh your options and research into the topic more before deciding which best fits you and your project. Until you've signed with an agent, you can always switch up your approach, too—for instance, you might try to seek an agent for a year and then decide to submit on your own, or vice versa.

When it comes to matching my writing to literary markets, I've always been my own advocate. I research publishers and hand-pick 'em, and I cheerfully do all of the preparation, networking, communication with publishers and editors, and submitting. I invest a few hours each month to the submission process.

That said, I'm always open to the option of getting an agent on a project-by-project basis someday. **A good agent has insider connections** and can get your book out of the slush pile and directly to an editor's attention, pronto. Some publishers only accept submissions from agent recommendations, so if you have an agent your book has a shot if submitted through the agency that it otherwise wouldn't.

A good agent also can negotiate for much more money and better contract terms in general because of their business experience. They are keenly aware of how your book fits (or doesn't) into the current hierarchy of what sells and also what has sold well in the past—**they can bypass oodles of markets that would be a waste of time and zero in on publishing fits. They can energize your career with perspectives on the business side of writing and suggest literary possibilities and ambitions you might not have envisioned yet.**

Good agents are well-respected professionals in their field who can give invaluable advice to writers about moves to make for long-term publishing careers. They are passionate advocates who believe in your writing and want to sell your book to a perfect-fit publisher. Who wouldn't value that?

Here's the thing, though: competition is fierce [understatement alert] and as with anything good, it requires much effort, time, and care for no guaranteed outcome. For three or four different book projects, I searched for an agent, researched agency guidelines, and thoroughly prepared proposals and manuscript samples. One project I submitted to over forty agents without a single bite. For two of my projects, I happily received a bunch of requests for more material ("a partial"), and three or four invitations to read the whole manuscript. Woot! Each time I proposed a book to an agent it was a labor-intensive process that ate up gobs of time. Yet, I also learned a ton about the submission process, sharpened my pitching and summarizing abilities, and got ever closer to understanding where my writing fit within the larger literary ecosystem, making the process well worth the effort. In the end, the three or four agents who genuinely liked my writing all ended up passing on my books for a variety of good reasons I understand now.

Those four projects remain unpublished; I pulled them from circulation because, honestly, the new work I'd penned in the intervening months and years was way stronger and more interesting anyway. You win some, you lose some. Onward!

I blame no one in this scenario. Not the quality of my writing (although it did get better over time and, with some luck, continues to) and certainly not the agents themselves. Agents don't possess clairvoyance or magic wands. **Like creative writing teachers, editors, and writers in your critique group, they cannot one hundred percent guarantee that your book will be sold or that readers will appreciate it once it is sold, even though it's beautifully written and grammatically in great shape.** Judgment of writing can be subjective at best and based on several competing factors, including the pressure cooker of time, subject or genre preferences, industry trends, reader preferences, and energy or monetary limits.

In fact, I've known more than one writing acquaintance who signed with literary agencies, had a respectable few-year match with an agent, and then amicably parted ways with their agent when the book did not sell. The writers later either self-published their manuscript or placed it with a university or small press. They still published and established a readership; it just ended up becoming a more circuitous route than planned (like so much in life).

That's right: signing with an agent is reason to celebrate and a great nod to your talent, but it *doesn't* promise that your book will be published.

How could this happen? Look, there are only so many agents reading work and only so many publishing slots at book publishers. Many publishers receive hundreds (or more!) of manuscripts and proposals per year but, alas, only have resources to publish a handful. **With or without agents, most people will be rejected. Let me repeat that: most people will be rejected. It's just a numerical reality when so many writers compete for a dozen or fewer publishing slots. I know, massive bummer.**

Clearly, with these odds, stellar work gets passed over and remains unsold for years all of the time! It's a business model, not an artistic one. An agent wants to sell your book but can do so only when a publisher is interested in it. Think of it as supply and demand: if the literary marketplace doesn't want a book about crafting wooden widgets, then your well-written book about making them won't sell no matter how much your agent and you believe in it.

Through no fault of the agent who tried to sell the client's book, nobody was interested at that time. Also notice that phrase: *at that time.* **Take heart: the literary landscape continues to evolve. Also, realizing the steep competition, you can redouble your efforts and determination, bringing your fiercest A-game to each manuscript pitch.**

I root for students and clients who seek agents and hope that they place all of their books with publishers who make their book dreams come true. **If getting an agent appeals to you, go**

for it. I think it's always worth a shot. Don't let anything discourage or dissuade you; agents still obviously acquire books all of the time and sell them, and your book could very well be one of them. **Do your research of agents' preferences and recently-sold projects, and then dive into preparing yours (read on for helpful tips below). I believe in big dreams; we learn, clarify, and grow from chasing them**.

Before you submit to agents make sure to increase your odds of getting a yes by doing most, if not all, of the following:

- Read agents' personal and/or agency website(s) and social media information to get a sense of the precise tone, content, and marketing of their recently-sold books and their work with clients.

- Peruse the websites of the writers they represent as well, noticing the publishers of the books to get an idea of the agents' connections in the publishing world as well as how your book would fit into their catalogs.

- Buy and/or library borrow some of their clients' books for a closer read.

- Read blogs published by agents or their agencies; they often post in plain sight online superb tips about preferred manuscript or proposal formatting and also agents' wish lists for the kinds of projects they eagerly seek but possibly haven't received yet.

- Ask around for the experiences of authors who've had agents; experiences and advice on this matter can vary and it's helpful to get as full a picture as possible before deciding what's best for your book.

- Read a book and/or attend a seminar or online class with more tips specifically tailored to submitting to agents.

- While you're at it, ask your creative writing teacher(s) or mentor for their advice about the agent-submission process, too.

Never cold-ask an agent (or a publisher, either); always research them and present yourself as the writing professional you are. Name-drop books they've worked on and give titles or author names for work that relates to yours in style, tone, and/or content. Don't do this in a disingenuous or slapdash way—put in the time, care, and thought to research and then demonstrate how you've written the book that matches their readers' tastes. Agents (and their staff) look for this kind of attention to detail and preparation.

And give yourself plenty of rewrites of the required materials you need to present with your submission. I spent three weeks working on just the two-page synopsis of one of my novels, bouncing the draft off of no less than three writing friends as I sculpted it. I've had students and clients work on their query letter for double that. It takes however long it takes.

Speaking of which: **when you figure in your interest level for getting an agent, factor in the key element of time.** I don't just mean the time it will take to encapsulate your whole project in compressed language and present it in its best light. **I mean the time you will spend learning this skill: seeking an agent, like seeking publication from literary magazines and like writing your book, is its own art form with highly-specialized rules, vocabulary, etiquette, expectations, and time frames.** There's a reason why there are whole classes, webinars, craft books, and blogs devoted to agents.

Treat it as a learning curve you're investing in, and prepare to power through setbacks or tiredness. Realize going in that it will not be an overnight process. With a bit of basic math, a writer could easily spend two or three years writing/workshopping/revising a book, another two or three years finding an agent, another year or two before a publisher buys the book, and then another year or two before it's edited, printed, and sent to readers. Scarily, that's how eight or nine years dissolve without noticing it. You probably don't want to wake up one morning and think, "Do I even *like* this book anymore? Why am I doing this? When is anybody other than my critique partner going to get to read this thing?" **Think about how much time you feel comfortable investing in approaching agents. For some writers, that's a few months while for others it's more than a year. For still others, it's until they get a yes.**

One way to cut down on the time it takes to get published is to submit the manuscript yourself to small presses, university presses, or indie houses. These three branches of publishing have passionate folks who care deeply about literature and yes, they also want to sell books and fiercely advocate your work. Indie, small, and university presses also tend to take chances on hybrid and innovative work and passion projects that might not mesh with the hottest current genres but which will connect with a diverse, enthusiastic readership.

If you choose to submit your work unsolicited (on your own, without an agent), research the presses with the same gusto you would apply to looking for agents. Read their website content and their social media posts. Order books from their catalog to get a good understanding of what they love to publish and to support their presses.

Also realize that many publishers only hold open submission periods for a certain calendar window each year; find out their manuscript deadline and submit only during that window (otherwise, your work could go unread and get an automatic rejection). It's well worth noting, too, that many small presses (just like many agents) don't want simultaneous submissions (work in consideration at other publishers); always check guidelines to see if the market allows simultaneous submissions before sending work to more than one publisher at the same time.

Both big and small presses share the same ultimate goal as agents: to craft and publish art while making profits. That said, realize that the remuneration (read: $$$) is often much reduced for small presses, which don't do advances, for instance. Indie and university presses often have fewer and smaller print runs or print-on-demand compared to big-name, large traditional publishers. They tend to run on enthusiasm and time investment with far less financial resources to invest. But invest they still will—not only in editorial and publishing and marketing resources and networking on your book's behalf (which definitely sells books) but in belief in you as a writer and in your book. Priceless! All of the publishing professionals at Vine Leaves Press have been top-notch, enthusiastic, and deeply invested in my books reaching as many readers as possible. That's the dream-team situation. I've received the level of care and marketing and editorial advice that benefits a writer's career.

Only you can decide how much energy and time you care to invest in each project and if seeking an agent or submitting directly to presses is the best path for your book. It's your decision whether that looks more like self-publishing to reach your readers directly, placing your book with an agent, at a large traditional house, or going the indie/small press route. **One is *not* better than the other. They all lead to the same place: publication.**

Factor in what feels right for your writing-career goals, the publishing marketplace, your schedule, your target audience, and each individual project's needs. Then go for it.

Decisions, Decisions: Choosing the Best Publication Fit for Your Book

Recently, I was really stewing over a hard career decision. I mean, this one was a conundrum and a whopper wrapped in a doozy.

Okay, not quite, but you get my drift. As I sat weighing pros and cons, I paused and asked myself: *If one of my nieces was approached with this situation and these circumstances and wanted to know my advice, what would I tell her?*

Bingo: sentences immediately started to pour out of my brain and onto the screen. I could barely type them fast enough. When I read them, I felt both centered and sure. Yep. That was it.

This nieces-focused question has served me remarkably well for the past few years. It cuts out all of the clutter in my head of others' potential reactions or unintended consequences and gets to the heart of the matter. I am invariably and unshakably in my nieces' corner and would only watch out for their best interests, whether they took the advice or not (and I never count on friends, family, or anybody *taking* advice after I've given it—they are free to do as they see fit).

For some reason, though, maybe it's being an introvert or an empath or an elder sister or a longtime teacher and editor, I've had trouble in the past making assertive moves without *first* considering the possible fallout for others. Since I was a small child, I have had the ability to foresee through reasoning and sidestep a lot of potential unpleasantness that way just by considering other people's viewpoints before deciding what to do.

As you can imagine, this outlook has been a help in some ways (I've had mostly harmonious interactions with students, clients, and friends) and simultaneously totally ridiculous in others (Hello, younger me: grow a backbone! You don't keep the world spinning. And you need to learn to sit in discomfort and not take on a boatload of guilt nor take other people's emotions or reactions personally. Go look in your own mirror: You're just one person and only in charge of yourself, thank you very much).

Moronic as it sounds, I'd sometimes line up decisions to take the fall-out *myself* rather than discomfort, anger, or inconvenience a student, client, friend, coworker, or family member.

Until my nieces were born. Now I keep that question handy for when I probably already know the answers I seek and the steps I need to take (thank you, life experience!) or the response I need to give but need that booster shot of no-nonsense courage to assert myself and do what's right for me at the time. **I've learned over and over the hard way: it's not selfish to represent your own needs.**

As writers, we have a million and one steps to take from first draft to finished book, and one of the biggest ones is deciding the right place to submit the prepared draft after editing.

The great news: with the internet, almost every publisher on the planet has a website. Their guidelines are easy to find as well as to check to see when their submission periods are open.

The bad news: almost every publisher on the internet has a website! You could easily make scrolling through the internet for publishers into a part-time job for a few weeks.

I've lost count of how many students and clients have asked me over the years: *how do you ever sort through them to find where to send your work?*

My top suggestions for finding a publisher that fits *your* specific manuscript:

Play favorites. Look up publishers who published your favorite recent nonfiction, especially craft books. You should be reading widely in the same genre(s) that you're writing. Keep a list of your favorites and check to see when these presses run open reading periods. Some only read during the school year (especially if they are a university press or a traditional publisher in NYC) and not during June-August, so keep that in mind.

Search a recent database or three. To quickly narrow down your options, I recommend that students peruse Submittable's free listings for book publishers and literary magazines under the Discover tab (you can find markets there using filters of key words, such as *nonfiction*) in their continuously updated listings of presses and publishers. *Poets & Writers Magazine* also has a splendid database for small press publishers (I found two of my own publishers there). Publishers Warehouse has a list of small presses that specifically publish reference books. NewPages also has a wonderful guide to many types of publishers seeking work. Include specific subject or theme key words as you search these databases to narrow down your options more quickly.

The wild card query. Keep in mind that some publishers who are open to nonfiction book manuscripts, such as memoirs or biographies, may also be open to other forms of nonfiction as well. The key to approaching a publisher with a query letter or email is to have studied the types of nonfiction they do publish to make sure it meshes with the tone and/or subject matter of your book and then to politely describe your book in a paragraph or two as well as your short, literary bio, and to inquire if they would be open to seeing more. This approach could work well for a small press (but be prepared not to hear for several weeks or months—small presses run on heart and passion but tend to be overworked and inundated with queries and submissions). I probably wouldn't approach a large traditional publishing house in this manner just because they tend to be much more stringent about the work they want to see cross their desks.

Magnificent niches. There are many stellar presses who publish specific demographics of writers who just might be a perfect match for your book. There are book markets who love to publish underrepresented voices such as minority authors, immigrant authors, as well as presses devoted to equal representation of every gender and sexuality, women writers, authors from certain geographic locales or cultures/subcultures, and authors who belong to certain social groups (such as sororities/fraternities, religious organizations, social justice groups, and myriad more). As you search for publishers, consider how your book might well already fit into these passionate presses' catalogs.

Big fish in a small pond or small fish in a big pond? I encourage my students and clients to consider their personality types as well as their goals for their books. As a writer, do you envision yourself being content to publish at a small press where you don't get an advance, but you might get more personal attention from your editors and possibly more promotion from the publisher because they publish fewer books per year? Or would you rather go with a known, big name where you might get an advance and/ or a two-book contract but perhaps not get as much contact from the staff who work there? There's no right or wrong answer to either question, and neither type of publishing is better. Base your answers on your work style as well as what you most hope to get out of the experience of working with professionals at either type of publisher. Know your own comfort level and what would mesh with your specific project.

Don't forget the super indie or the uni options: You know who is often included in small presses but not specifically talked about in that category as often? Two kinds of publishers: the independent/indie presses and the university-based presses. Some indie presses run on even smaller budgets than their big-cousin small presses. They may be a new press or run out of a home office or affiliated with an author who self-published and now wants to expand their range to help publish one or two other authors' books. There's a lot to be said for the passion of the indie publisher. The zine scene of the '80s and '90s came out of this kind of one-person-makes-a-difference gusto, and the ease of internet communication makes it easier to contact the folks who launch an indie press and query about their publishing preferences.

A lot of indie presses might have just one or two employees who already work full-time jobs and have families or other responsibilities and may only be able to publish a handful or fewer books per year. Don't discount them, however—they are still professionals who seek quality work to publish and, in my experience, often very open to querying about a project. Be patient about waiting for a response (let at least a few weeks go by before sending a follow-up email; they likely got your first query and are just running behind on answering messages—no biggie).

University presses are affiliated with colleges and institutes of higher education, sometimes high schools but most often grad and university MA and MFA and even PhD programs. These presses frequently represent a wide array of nonfiction (and poetry and/or fiction) titles, many exploring important social issues and/or academic disciplines. Often, both highly-published professors and students learning the publishing ropes and/or who have already had meaningful experiences on both sides of the publishing desk comprise the editorial staff. These folks, too, are passionate about the written word and well-worth querying.

Ask a writing friend. I've learned about a few presses through my fellow writing pals that I otherwise probably wouldn't have found on my own. Ask someone who writes in the same genre who they're reading and what their favorite nonfiction publishers are. You just never know who you'll discover next through such informed minds.

Consider setting aside a few mornings or afternoons for researching and bookmarking publishers that possibly match for the genre and tone you've written, especially as you edit and as your draft nears completion.

With the diversity of wonderful publishers out there, there's bound to be a press that is seeking just what you've written, or perhaps you'll decide to self-publish.

Proceed to the next chapter for tips about the latter exciting publishing option.

Grow Your Own Success: Adventures in Self-Publishing

I've always liked the natural sciences. All of the "hard" sciences, like physics and chemistry and engineering, with their math-heavy equations and pinching rules about what has to go where when, turn me cold as an icicle, mostly because I find them inscrutable and stubborn. The earth sciences, though, speak to me where I reside—in potential, patience, personal investment, growth, and the kind of everyday magic that sneaks up on you.

One of my favorite "experiments" when I was in elementary school was growing crystals. My mom mixed together some kind of homemade concoction that she'd read about in a kid's book from the library—it seems in the murk of my memory that baking soda was somehow involved in the swirl within the kitchen mixing bowls, but I might be misremembering. It was some kind of baking ingredient that came in a small cardboard drum. A dash of this, a splash of that, some blue and red food coloring to make purple and a ruddyish pink in the red spectrum, and we took turns spinning the stuff around and around.

The anticipation was part of the process—as was the work of creating. I recall dipping the wet substance onto strings that dripped down our fingers as we then dangled the strings from half-used pencils that we didn't plan on using for a while. As a protective bell jar, we used an upturned glass tumbler for Sister's and an upturned canning jar for mine.

It certainly wasn't instantaneous or even within a week that we saw results. But we'd check every day after school, gazing up at the top of the upright piano that was our great-grandmother's and our platform for showing off our in-progress science project.

And one day, shazam! The frilly formations had appeared. That first fuzzy bud of quartzy mineral draped over the pencil top was deeply satisfying. We found more and more reasons to check on the crystals' progress during the mornings and evenings and weekends, monitoring each frill and speculating on how big they'd get.

Grow, grow, grow—it was happening! But it couldn't be rushed. It took however long it took, and that was that.

I thought about this recently as I bought my nieces crystal-growing kits. I think about those crystals now and again as I teach a course in publishing for a popular online Master's program. As I offer tips on the various ways to reach publication for one's writing projects, self-publishing is one of the many viable options we discuss at our class discussion boards.

Much like growing crystals back in the day, **self-publishing *isn't* a shortcut. It still involves quite a few steps** (mostly the same steps as you'd experience after getting an acceptance letter from either a traditional or small-press publisher). The major difference is that, instead of getting the expertise of a bevy of assigned editors (from an acquisitions editor to a developmental editor to a copy editor) and having a timeline and publication date laid out before you and some professionals to bounce questions off of, **you're going to take on the mantle of all of these steps yourself, harnessing your passion for your project, your natural skills, and possibly the hired help of some editors along the way.**

It used to be that self-publishing was considered the low-brow or no-talent option. Not so at all today! Self-publishing can be wonderful for authors ready to buckle up and put in the care and learning curve it takes to make their books successful.

I've had several talented writing friends, clients, and students who self-published—and one of my literary friends lives off of the sales of her series. That's right—unlike ninety-nine percent of the rest of my publishing peeps, she makes her bread and butter from sales of her books: she's frugal; knows her target audience; is tremendously focused, hard-working, talented, and media-savvy; and writes in a lucrative genre—super impressive! She continually impresses and motivates me.

Even my pals who keep day jobs and can't live off royalties, though (as the vast majority of us writers), *can* self-publish and net readers and royalties like those who publish work through a press by putting in a lot of legwork—also impressive!

So, what changed in publishing in the past decade or so? E-publishing! The internet has opened up ways for writers to directly market to readers/consumers. Writer-reader interactions are a key element to building a target audience for ebooks (and print books, too). The internet also offers free publishing platforms and social-media channels for building fan bases who, if they buy your first book and like it, are likely to buy your second and so on. This trend has taken publishing from being a gatekeeper situation to an open lawn anyone can stand on if they'd like.

What skills and outlook help self-published authors flourish?

• Do you have superb self-motivation?

- Great at managing your time and getting work done?

- Focus well?

- Already actively building your platform, such as your website, blog, and/or social media?

- Network in person and via email/text like a champ?

- Do you find numerous steps and near-constant decision-making energizing rather than overwhelming?

- Are you willing to skip the pitching and/or submission process and pour the gusto you'd put into query letters, book proposals, and sharpening your opening chapter directly into editing (on your own or with a hired professional), formatting/uploading (again, on your own or with a freelancer), and marketing your brainchild in numerous ways and with frequency?

- Do you have a project that is a very specific niche that agents and editors might find difficult to market within their current catalog but you feel passionate about?

Then self-publishing could be a marvelous option for your project!

With self-publishing, you get to decide all of your publishing and marketing strategies—from book length to the cover reveal to preordering to launch day and giveaways. It's your baby, and you're running this show! **Who loves your project and knows its needs better than you do? Likely: nobody!**

If you're a big-picture thinker who can also drill down deeply into detail, much the better. There are about a thousand moving puzzle pieces to self-publishing and marketing, and some authors find learning this skill so freeing that they start their own publishing imprints to help other authors either self-publish or publish within their own small presses after launching their own books. **It's a world of possibility!**

That said: be honest with yourself. How much time do you have to read up on, figure out/practice, and put into motion with your particular project all of the moving pieces that it takes to prepare, publish, and launch a book? Only you can answer this question.

What are some reasons for potentially putting a pause on self-publishing? If you are in school full-time, or training at a new job, or have three part-time jobs, are the primary care-giver for young children or elderly parents, are committed to running a small business, lead numerous groups within your community, or know that you have organizational or energy challenges that make completing everyday tasks challenging enough to power through, **then sit down and consider what in your life you can feasibly trim back or get help with to make self-publishing a reality for you.**

If the answer is nothing-right-now, then it doesn't mean self-publishing isn't an option for your project (you can still read up on it and prepare for the future when you will have more time)—it just means that you realize the dedication and time involved in self-publishing and at this time your resources and energy are already spoken for.

That said, I've known students who had several of these life circumstances and either still self-published but extended the time it took to meet their goals to avoid getting overwhelmed or they waited a few weeks or months to begin when their schedules lightened.

Another popular reason for not wishing to self-publish: a writer who sees the investment in the publishing tasks as time that they could instead spend on the more-creative act of writing. Understandable. Publishing is its own time-consuming art.

Good news: keep in mind, too, that it's not an all-or-nothing decision. One of the most exciting things about the current publishing landscape is that you can mix or match your publishing options, based

on each project. You might decide to submit your project to some small presses or traditional publishers or agents first, to see if you get any interest, and then a few months or a year down the line decide to give self-publishing a try and find that you enjoy the process. Or, you might small-press publish one project and self-publish another. Or publish with a university press or indie press for a book or two. Or, you might dip your toes into the waters of self-publishing with a short story or novella rather than a full-length collection. Some authors choose to self-publish a small project and give it away for free (or nearly free) to strengthen and build their target audience, meanwhile learning layout, editing, and publishing skills that they will adjust and apply to self-publishing their full-length manuscripts later.

You have options—plenty of them!

Whatever form(s) of publishing you decide fits you and your project, **author involvement in publishing and marketing is crucial to the success and sales of your book.**

Rejection: the Obligatory Chapter on Everyone's "Favorite" Topic

"When my clients get discouraged, I say: 'Honey, you haven't even *tasted* rejection. Wait'll I tell you about my writer friend.'"

It's a winter Sunday evening and, thanks to COVID-19, my pal and I sit at home, catching up on the phone for forty-five minutes—a welcomed respite that we rarely take since we both run small businesses.

Her bright laughter is a return to my youth. Also, the fact that this talented woman I've known for more than half of my life has just validated my writing journey—with its ups, downs, and sideways spins—reminds me that I'm still striving and thriving.

"So what number are you up to now?" she asks, with interested mischievousness in her voice that reminds me of when we were kids.

I grab my writer's submission notebook from my desk. "I just submitted #1,287 last week. So that hovers me somewhere in the vicinity of 337 yeses and, um … around 950 rejections."

She whistles, and we laugh again.

950 rejections. Staggering. A part of me is glad I didn't know that number when I started submitting regularly (at least three times, often more, a month) back in 2000.

Now, that number is just my writing rejections; it doesn't factor in the multitude of friendship, relational, and job rejections I've experienced concurrently in the intervening years. Over a ten-year period, I had a surpassing knack for getting second-runner-up after job interviews and then being told with smiles that I *almost* got the gig. (Dear HR people everywhere: please encourage your staff *never* to leak this information post-interview. Even if they think it's encouraging to the applicant; it's not. Better they think they're the fifth than the runner-up who gets the *we-really-really-liked-you-but-we-went-with-the-other-candidate* spiel. Ick.)

Readers perusing my book covers' bios or looking at my website and social media have no clue of the day-to-day slogging; they see the highlight reel. All of the practicing and publishing artists I know have an online highlight reel—it's part of putting oneself out there and promoting our finished work. People who don't write professionally probably think I just wrote the book as easily as Athena sprang fully-formed out of Zeus' head, passed it over for publication, and voilà!: a published book a few weeks later. If only! Each book is more like at least a three-year chunk of my life from first draft to holding the published book, if not longer. One of my poetry books was a five-year chunk, from start to first, second, third drafts to organizing into sections to submitting again and again to acceptance and then more editing and, finally, publication.

Granted, I'm not complaining about the time investment. **You have to spend your life invested in something meaningful (often, many somethings) and I want to spend mine on subjects I have a genuine passion for. It's vital for writers, though, to prepare for the time and energy investment each book-length project requires.**

The fact that readers don't know a lot about the publication process is as it should be, though. The perseverance necessary to become a published author is highly personal and, honestly, running around telling people who don't practice an art just how horrendous it is to be bombarded with rejections doesn't accomplish a bunch but tire out both teller and listener and invite people to tell you to quit. During a down period, some people delight in coaxing others to quit things that usually light them up inside. **Never give people free rent space in your head to encourage you to quit something you love.**

But among fellow practitioners of craft and aspiring published authors, I want to keep it real—no, realer than real, let's say. I want to save you the crippling self-doubt that can come from expecting an easy, quick sale. **I want you to know straight-up *not* to expect a "one and done."** That is, don't think that each manuscript or project you submit will find a publication home or agent straight out of the gate; that's exceedingly rare (lightning in a bottle) and, in my experiences and those of my students and clients, usually happens after years of writers putting in their dues. Expect more like ten, twenty, or even forty submissions and done.

Or maybe more. I know of an already-published acquaintance who submitted a very well-written, long-workshopped memoir over fifty times before she landed a well-deserved contract. I've also known authors who got acceptance letters and were in the midst of working with an editor only to have the press either suddenly go out of business, their editor or agent leave and the ensuing editor/agent not want their project, or the press decides not to publish their work due to budget cuts. Their books went right back to square one: submitting it again to the slush pile. Ouch, and it happens.

A lot of beautiful and articulate prose gets rejected for numerous reasons (such as that the press just published a similar book or they don't believe they can sell your book to their target audience or they just didn't connect with your wonderful book as much as so-and-so's wonderful book). **Most of these reasons have nothing to do with the quality of your work or its readability and publishability. Believe that. Don't let it stop you.**

Still, I know the bitter bite of rejection after rejection on the same project is exhausting, so **here are a few proactive suggestions I make to my writing students and clients who support long-haul, career-building success:**

ABW: Always Be Writing. Don't put all of your eggs in one basket. I've known writers who work on a single project for eight or nine years (or more) without publishing. Years! One project! That's putting an awfully lot of pressure on one book to succeed and can wilt writers, even if they have amazing writing chops. **While you're working on your reference book, set it aside every few days or weeks to write something else, something shorter**, say: a short story, a poem, a flash fiction, or a personal essay of under 2,000 words.

ABS: Always Be Sending. Start to submit these smaller pieces, even while you work away on the chapters in your reference book. Not only will you continue to grow as a writer of these smaller pieces, but you will inject something else back into your writing: fun! Along with a shot of

imagination that can get lost easily in the big picture of writing a longer work.

I work on about four projects simultaneously—two main/longer ones, and then a lot of little poems or flash fictions or essays or photos in-between that I submit each month. That might not be an optimal work-flow for other writers, which I completely respect. Even one poem or a short story now and again in addition to consistently working on a book adds up over a year or two and renews a writer's process. Diversify whenever possible.

The stand-alone striver. You can always take a chapter from your book that reads well on its own and submit it as an essay to literary magazines before your whole book is ready for submission.

Little ain't loser. I broke into submitting to agents and publishers through all of the practice I had submitting and publishing in indie, small, and university magazines—those skills transfer beautifully to submitting larger projects. Many writers rack up publications *first* in literary magazines or small indie presses or on online blogs which they then include on their cover letters when they approach publishers of book-length manuscripts later.

Just as importantly, these publication credits also boost an author's confidence—there's magic in seeing your name in a byline or having a reader email or text their appreciation out of the blue. **This is also a stellar way to start building your target audience.**

Keep in mind, as with publishing a book-length work, that most work submitted to literary magazines also gets rejected on the regular (sometimes more than seventy-five percent of manuscripts for each issue!), so **when you get a rejection, keep submitting elsewhere. It's wonderful practice in both persistence and in writing a cover letter that presents your work professionally each time you submit your shorter pieces.**

Look for the newbies. Take a chance on new publications. Yes, everyone wants the big names, but in my experiences first- and second-issue journals have enthusiastic editors raring to promote your work on social media. They are also much more willing to work with untapped, up-and-coming talent. Even as a highly published author, I submit a few times a year to any literary magazine that looks promising, even a premiere issue. Ultimately, our goal is for an ever-widening audience to read us—newbies are marvelous for this and for their passion for promoting literature. Win-win.

Make your creation space inviting. I thoroughly believe we writers deserve our own space. Seek out that tiny spot, even if it's a corner of your basement or guest room or one little wooden desk built in the 1900s like mine is, and make it your very own. Adorn your space with attractive folders and pens in myriad colors if that's your jam and notebooks that call you to jot ideas. Or action figures from when you were a kid. Or Christmas twinkle lights. This space is *yours*, after all. Choose a comfy chair, 'cause you'll be sitting there a while—although your space will be so appealing that you won't think about the time passing as you type.

Make your writing space a positive production zone physically as well as emotionally. A cool novelist friend on the West Coast sent me an encouraging postcard six months ago with a typewriter and a motivating writing quote. I immediately propped the card against my stained-glass lamp and it pumps me up to get writing each time I see it throughout the day. You could do the same with photos from a magazine or printed-out quotes from your favorite authors to get you jazzed to work each day. It's not rocket science—**it's the kind of small attention to detail we can align that makes a big difference as we ready ourselves to write.**

Much as we probably don't think of it as such: writing is almost as physical an art as it is intellectual and emotional. Make your physical space reflect what your writing self most wants to express verbally. Keep it can-do.

Mindset adjustments, midstream. Bottom line: sometimes we all get down on ourselves and our work. It's perfectly normal, especially in fallow periods where the writing feels all uphill and nobody seems interested in what we make.

We just *can't stay* in that slog perpetually. Here's what keeps me going through my glum times: I remind myself that I keep wanting to make it happen. This writing life has been my dream since before I could form my letters and I still wake up wanting more of it every day. I was born to connect through communication, writing, and publishing: I believe that soul-deep.

Check-in with your gut and your own motivations now and again. Visualize that rare person or thing *you'd do anything to nourish and to see grow*. It might be your best friend or child or niece/nephew/nibling or grandchild or lover or a charity you have a passion for promoting or marathon running or the bakery you co-founded or fill-in-the-blank. *Now, when and how would you give up on that person or thing? Oh, you wouldn't, would you, even when circumstances wore on you?* **That's the level of determination to apply to your writing, editing, and publishing efforts.**

You have something only you can say on the page. That's the level of gusto I've seen in all of my published friends and students. **When you want it *that diligently* you will make it happen. Over and over again. You've got this.**

Advice for Hiring an Editor

As a freelancer, I love it when a talented client writes to me with a promising project to edit. While not all projects will fit into my schedule or editing specializations, I take on as many projects I believe in as I can offer quality feedback on per year.

But what about from the other side of the desk: the writer seeking an editor? What should authors keep in mind when finding an editorial fit for their nonfiction book?

Know what kind of editing you're interested in and ask for it specifically. Many writers approach editors without sharing the specific type of editing they seek. If you have a general idea, you'll get a more-accurate price estimate and possibly save you and your potential editor time in email tag figuring it out along the way. Win-win.

Since freelancers book projects weeks or even months ahead of time, knowing the specific kind of help you seek will provide a much more accurate estimate of when the editor can schedule your project and how much turn-around time to expect.

There are three main kinds of editing most freelancers offer: **copy edits, developmental edits, and proofreading.** Copy editors search for inconsistencies and grammatical errors and awkward sentences/run-ons, to name just three areas of feedback you can expect to get. Developmental editors, on the other hand, prove a big-picture deep-dive into your book's structure and literary elements, from chapter organiza-tion, lack of transitions, areas where you should flesh the text out or include specific examples, characterization (for novels), pacing, and more. Also, developmental editors brainstorm and are quite helpful if you're working on an early draft and hope to flesh out your material. (You have probably already correctly guessed that, out of the three types of editing I do, developmental projects snatch my heart.)

Developmental editing takes more time, in general, than copy editing or proofreading, so it usually costs more. Proofreading tends to be the cheapest form of editing and the most surface-polishing. Proofreading is usually the very last process of editing a text before it heads to press and doesn't include comments on structure, development of key ideas, expanding analysis, or inconsistencies.

Each form of editing has a different price tag based on the amount of feedback involved and the experiences of the editor—many editors charge either by page or by word.

Expect to pay slightly more for a long-time editor or someone who works for a publisher, compared to those just starting out. If you're looking for bargains or want to give a newbie editor a chance, that could be great...or it could turn out to be a terror. **Exercise due diligence in checking around for opinions before hiring any editor.**

Consider going in the kind of editing you feel comfortable with as well as what your budget is.

Check out an editor's webpage and the books they've worked on. House styles of publishers can vary widely and so can editorial preferences. Prepare yourself with as much information as you can about the editor's projects and personal style (even the way they list the copy on their website, especially in their bio, will give you big clues to their editorial style and voice) *before* writing them an email.

I know this will be unpopular with many younger authors, but please: **I don't recommend approaching editors by text** *unless* they list being open to that very informal style of communication. Also, always proofread your email before contacting any editor to look as polished and serious about you craft as possible.

While you're there at an editor's website or social media posts, see if they have their rates posted. Some editors do, some don't. **You can ask politely**—after *first* introducing your book, your word count and genre, your website or social media, the kind of editing you're seeking, and your request for further information, of course. **Editors care about getting queries that include more information than a single sentence. As an editor, authors who include links to their websites with writing samples and/or more information about them and their craft always pique my interest more than cold queries.**

Network it! I get sixty percent of my editing gigs from satisfied customers. Ask around. Who do your professors, writing friends, and published writers in your local communities hire for freelance editing? Even if the writers you've met have worked with an editorial team assigned to them via a publishing company, many companies list their editorial staff on their website. You could write to an editor, introducing yourself and your project very briefly, to see if they have editorial colleagues or contacts who offer freelance editing.

Editors are a tight bunch and often recommend each other, especially for quality jobs. Make sure you send a quality email query by making it succinct, detailed, and proofread, including the suggested elements above.

Dot your i's and cross your t's. In other words bring your A-game. I love it when authors show me their enthusiasm for their projects through the care they take describing their projects. When an author is jazzed about their book and prepared for the next steps, it sparkles off of the screen; that's an author I want to work for.

I cannot stress this enough: **before you approach any editor, have your details in a row. Prepare a one-paragraph synopsis/ description about your book that you email and at least a chapter of your writing (usually the first chapter) that you offer to show the editor so they can decide if they will take on your manuscript.**

Like authors, editors often specialize. Say your book is about how to write a science fiction novel that sells, but the editor has a specialty in romance and westerns. That editor might not be familiar with the tropes of science fiction and might not be the right person for developmental editing or copy edits for this particular project.

Stay open to making new connections and/or getting recommendations to fit your project best.

Try this exercise:

Write a one- or two-paragraph description of your book that encapsulates the main ideas in your book, your target audience, and your writing style. Show this succinct synopsis to a writing friend or two for suggestions before using it in querying emails to potential editors.

Marketing 101: Tips Aplenty

Guess what the top two most-dreaded topics are for the writers I teach? Hint: we've already covered one: that stink bomb, rejection. Can you guess the other? That's right, sales: AKA: marketing. Oh, the dreaded dud topic on how to hustle one's intellectual brainchild like an orphan left on a doorstep!

I'm with you: idea-brainstorming, creating, developing/fleshing out, rearranging, and even editing way surpass glee levels for me on the joy-o-meter of writing a book. Marketing, not nearly.

It's only natural that, as a creative force, that we much prefer the more personal, individual-based making process to the other-focused, networking aspects that can start to feel either like begging for business or slightly embarrassing bragging. Either way, definitely time-draining and it can stretch even the most cheerful writer out of their comfort zone and into the fray where, as an artiste, they loath to be.

But it's a necessary "evil." Think of it from the other side of the desk: who wants to publish a book that doesn't sell? Who wants to invest time, energy, money, and effort into an author who won't even pony up to invest their own additional sweat equity (time, intellect, networking, and enthusiasm) into their project to make it a success? Nobody!

Publishers expect authors to be self-motivated when it comes to spreading the word and getting our work out there for their monetary, time, and networking efforts. It's only fair that we authors contribute to our books' success.

All gloom and doom? Nope: good news—it's never been easier to connect with readers. You don't need a ton of money to promote your work effectively, and over time spreading the word gets easier as your network increases.

Whether you self-publish or publish with a small, university, indie, or traditional large press, myriad possibilities await for getting your book into the hands of readers. No need to go red with embarrassment or to lose sleep at night about sales (please don't—just keep expanding your reach and your target audience as you go).

It doesn't mean sell-out your artistic soul; it *does* mean *actively participate.*

Here are more than twenty strategic marketing tips I've either used or my writing clients and students have used to successful sales

Guest blog on a literary site or two. If you do a great job, they'll ask you back near your book launch or shortly after, or you can approach them with the idea of guesting again at a time close to your book release. Guest blogging is fun and often increases a writer's audience.

Do a cover reveal at your website and/or social media a few weeks or months before the release of your book to drum up excitement.

Take part in a blog crawl or book-release event, online or in your home community.

Offer book giveaways or prizes.

Join sites specifically aimed at readers, like **Goodreads.**

Get your book reviewed on sites that sell books. Readers often do peruse reader comments before deciding to buy. If your publisher gives advance review copies, take advantage of that to line up reviews. Send a potential "deadline" for the review and a friendly reminder close to the time if the review hasn't been posted. If your reviewers also write, offer to give reviews in kind for their books.

Branch out. If your book has a special topic, such as my book *Photography for Writers,* you can advertise and/or write guest blogs or articles for a literary magazine or site and then mention your book in the article. Also, take out ads in subject-related magazines—I bought ads in three photography-related magazines to advertise my book and expand my readership.

Make sure to update your contributor's bio; it's easy to forget to include your book and a link to where to purchase it, and what a loss—when literary magazines publish other pieces, the contributor's bio is a free chance to pitch your book to new potential readers.

Cross-promote: agree to post about a friend's book on your social media in exchange for their posting about your book. This is a friendly way to show support for your fellow authors' books while also extending your reach to their network. Win-win.

Send out snail-mail postcards. Old-school? Yes, but that can be charming and grab readers' attention—I still remember three authors (and their books) who sent me snail-mail postcards in the past few months (and I purchased all three books). It's an initial expense that may well boost sales.

Guest on a podcast or start your own writing podcast.

Create a private social-media group for literary interests and writers.

Buy ads at literary magazines, both online and in print.

Make short book trailer videos to post online.

Repost all of your publisher's posts and videos about your book on your own page/account.

Post short videos on writing topics and mention/plug your book.

Start a (quarterly) newsletter/news blast that goes out to your subscription or contact list(s), with updates on your writing, your social media/website links, as well as some meaningful freebies for readers—sometimes I include a new prompt or article I write just for my newsletter subscribers. I used to send out my newsletters via email six or seven times a year; now I send one out quarterly, about three to five times a year max to writers who have taken my classes and/or expressed interest in my writing projects and books.

Participate in an in-person reading, both to launch your book and afterwards.

Get in touch with any schools you attended—many host special readings once or twice a year for alums who have written books.

Participate in an open-mike at a bookstore or coffee shop—bring your book (and one or two that you might sell) and read an excerpt.

Schedule an online reading. One of the few positive aspects of COVID-19 quarantining has been the number of readings all over the country I've been able to attend from the comfort of home.

Commit to posting on social media with frequency. This might mean a few times a week, once a week, or bi-weekly, but make sure to keep posting. Readers who notice that writers' social media and/or blogs or websites are months, if not years, behind often express disappointment, and you miss out on sharing your latest project(s) and on possible sales. Keep your content fresh and up-to-date. Comment on others' social media posts, too, to spread the support to authors you appreciate.

Try this exercise:

Pick the three marketing methods above that speak to you the most. These will be the three ideas you'll set up and/or try first to get your marketing network on the move. You could start/begin several of these ideas as early as this week (such as starting an author page on social media, guest blogging, and making writing friends you'll cross-promote with once your book is ready).

As time goes on and you connect more with your target audience, you are welcome to pick additional methods from the list as you market. I started with two types of social media and now market in six or seven ways at once. Be patient, yet focused, when you begin.

The Bright Blue Flame, or:
Be the Tortoise

It's no secret: I'm a klutzy, horrible athlete with next-to-no interest in organized sports. I even often bump into the coffee table or other furniture when my head is in the clouds pondering something. I so admire paintings and the ability to draw, but the cats I've drawn look like monkeys and vice versa on the page and a caricature of my face that I draw for my nieces' cards is just about the extent of my realism visually. I dabble with crafts and collage once in a blue moon but don't have a real passion for it. I come from a very handy family of builders and I can't fix a blasted mechanical thing or build anything. Full disclosure: I sometimes have trouble putting batteries into the remote because I forget to align the + and − on the batteries to the correct spots and then wonder why the remote isn't working.

Writing, though. That's my bright blue inner flame. It always has been, since before I could even adequately draw each letter. My mom says I started to speak at three months old, and her jaw hit the floor because she never expected her kid to become verbal that young. I take every step possible to nurture that blue flame and the similar fires I see in my students and clients. There's a book or twenty burbling at any time, and I want to see them flare into reality.

When I love something and want to make that something flourish, I have endurance, follow-through in abundance, and patience that rivals a bulldog. I am no flake. If I'm going to do something, you can bet I'm completely invested. I play the long game with all of its twists and turns; I invite you to do the same.

Being a tortoise is not only fine, it's often the way to go in a writer's career. Like Aesop's famed turtle, put out of your mind the speedy bunnies who zoom towards their goals faster or who use underhanded moves—you're on your own path and you'll get there. Get busy focusing on your crawling; I mean, writing. Say what?!

Others will probably forget you're still quietly working over here. You'll just keep eating any obstacles for breakfast cereal, thank you. You'll keep going up, around, over, beside, and beyond those obstacles, getting closer and closer to your goals. These are the kind of writing students and clients I've seen succeed over the years.

I've seen a lot of writers bent on speed who burned out, gave up, or spent their careers complaining that everyone else got the breaks—**meanwhile, the slow burners just keep quietly and consistently making and sharing work.**

Now, this determination isn't easy coasting. Nope. You will slam up against some tender areas; you might have to make some adjustments. There are many relationships in life where we can't just make independent decisions. Even with our writing, most of us have day jobs or dependents or significant others, and their lives are just as important and need our affection and attention on a daily, sometimes hourly, basis. Being a writer isn't an open invitation to selfishness or ignoring connections or responsibilities in our lives.

That said: **people who genuinely love you will root for you. Don't prepare for a huge crowd, mind you, but there are encouragers everywhere** (you might be holding the book of one right this minute). There's the high-school teacher, for instance, who came to a Zoom reading one of my graduate students had for his published book last month—twenty-five-plus years after he was her student! There's the writing buddy or coach or colleague who compliments you on your writing or asks with genuine interest how it's going. Maybe your co-worker, Secret Santa, or father-in-law buys you a book about writing because they heard you're writing something.

These advocates, whether they write or not, will sustain you. They are worth their weight in gold—oh, praise them and send a thank you text or message or, even better, a handwritten thank you. These delightfully tuned-in people might not make the writing path easier, but they will be there for you to celebrate each little milestone of this path you take at your own pace, whether that's zippy or trudgy. You'll get there. Not as quickly as you'd planned more times than not, but it'll happen if you keep writing.

Truthfully, though, there will be many people who may likely drop out of your life (at least for a while) when you start to get this book written and tell them about it. Or you'll read the jealousy on their faces and wish you'd never said a thing and change the subject. I've been there. More than once.

You're making it happen, and this will trigger insecurities about what *they're not doing.* Your shine will make them feel shaded, and they'll think you are a braggart even if that's the very last thing on your mind—you just freaking want to share what you're making. They won't want to hear a drop of it. It's a giant downer, these moments; I totally get it. These are not your people.

Whether you choose to tell your companions or not is your decision. Sometimes I don't tell anyone, except for dear writing friends or family, until I'm ready to drop the projects—I don't need to give a peanut gallery of opinions free rent in my brain, thank you very much. Your steps (even tiny ones) towards your goal will rattle some colleagues and friends. Count on that. Sometimes those people will be your intimates and their body language or odd responses will shock or hurt you in the short run. These reactions will sting.

A man I once had a flirtation with replied to work I sent to him, as if jesting: "You're a force to be reckoned with." Reckoned with? Me-ouch. I'd hoped for camaraderie and connection and to make a positive impression that would inspire him to share his work in kind. Well, make an impression I did, but not the one I'd hoped. He either didn't notice or, likely, didn't care that I'm a vulnerable and gentle woman in many areas of my life, like everyone else. I'm not blocking anyone else's path to success by continuing to practice and share my art—none of us is. Quite the opposite.

A word about snarky comments from one artist to another: these compliments with daggers attached are deviously passive-aggressive and designed to distance. They can lodge like a clenched fist in the chest but do not accept them as representative of literary truth or the quality of your work. They are one person's opinion informed by whatever the judger is going through at that time. Period.

Yeah, I get it: such statements ultimately betray the insecurities of the sayer, but worse, they side-swipe and can potentially derail a fellow author's confidence for months, if not years. I understand the upset. While his comment in no way discouraged me from making projects or from sharing my work with other artists in the future, it certainly was a blip that left a bruise. I've never forgotten the deep disappointment: I'd dared to ask for the affection of the wrong audience and paid steeply for it.

There's little worse than a compliment with daggers attached. There's little worse than implying that, sure, a writer can be passionate and enthusiastic and unwavering, but the return will be the punishment of rejection from your target audience. **Don't do that to anyone else. Make every effort to make a positive path for fellow writers, even if their work isn't what you like or prefer to read.** If someone goes out of their way to share with you, the least you can do is make a safe space for them and their art.

Now, I realize such unexpected stings are almost a rite of passage and bound to happen to people who practice any art and share work. If you continue to try and get a scrap of success in your field, somebody somewhere will isolate you or have a smug comment about it. It's par for the course, although an unpleasant par.

But here's the gift in that kind of experience: yeah, it stings, but now you've got a story, you've got some adversary cachet, and you will continue to flourish. These haters have inadvertently switched on your determination light and let you know that you've got something special that was too sparkly for them. **You are wrong for that audience, but I can promise you others will appreciate and welcome your work. We all sometimes pick the wrong audience. It happens— grieve, observe, keep writing, and then pick a different audience.**

For every discourager who is reckless with their comments on your work, take heart: there's another person who will value what you're making and find the strength in your writing amazing, no daggers attached. It may take some trial and error to find your audience, but find them you will.

Bottom line: if you write, others will judge. No way around it. I don't know if it hurts worse from other artists or from colleagues and contemporaries without an artistic bone in their bodies. Criticism of any flavor is distasteful and a downer. I know, I know. It is hideous; most of us just want to hide, make our snarky asides in private, have a laugh, and be done with it. But **if you're an artist, you are doing a brave and radical thing: you are putting your inner**

world in the outer world. You're shining a spotlight on your thoughts and putting them on display. I repeat: others will judge you.

Just remember: what some people consider an off-putting force is, for others, a beautiful desire to fulfill your life's dreams with the resources you have. This takes guts and grit and a bit of humble self-restraint to start again and again. Add another again for good measure.

Be proud that you possess a dream or ten—so many people never did, or they had them, then life pulled them away, and they live in sinking regret.

Be prepared for pushback and push back on it. **Sharing your dreams and marveling at how far you've come isn't hubris or bragging: it's hope and hard work. No matter how anyone else reacts: you've earned the right to be proud of your work.**

This doesn't mean being aggressive about it or sending them your work once you're published to rub it in their faces or tagging them on social media. No, **this is a simple, quiet continuation of your work. You're just going to persevere is all—and is everything.**

I get it: until we have those people in our lives to champion us or while we're still making that core group of supporters, it's very tempting to give in, especially midstream, on writing a book.

Here's a foundational memory of my childhood that has kept me from giving up over a twenty-plus year career in publishing when things were bleak, bleak, bleak many times, even after the first few publications when I got a string of ten rejections or more in a row.

It was the mid-1980s. I sat on a front porch with a family friend and my parents one summer night. Crickets chirped in the fields beyond, and the farmer, a usually jovial man in his seventies who used to bring eggs from the farm and call me a funny nickname on Sunday nights when he'd stop by in his yellow truck, had just been diagnosed with terminal cancer.

To say that I'd never seen an adult weep like he wept is one hundred percent candid and still hits me in the gut. I was nine years old, and I looked down at the concrete porch where the kitten played one minute to the hanging petunia basket the next, with a knot in my stomach. My parents, in their early thirties, looked a little stunned, which was also confusing for a kid; they always seemed to know what to do and say. Not this time. They mostly listened and nodded in sympathy as he talked. For a long time. A time that felt like hours but was likely about forty-five minutes. One thing he said, on one of his last visits, has always echoed in my mind.

"If there's anything you want to do, don't wait," he sobbed. "Do it now. You have to do it now."

Now, there are oodles of things I half-heartedly wouldn't mind doing: learning how to dance better, take photographs in the Sangre de Cristo Mountains, get a residency at an arts colony, become fluent in French. Truthfully, though, if none of these things happen, I'm still living my best life and I won't regret it not happening.

But those things that I feel a burning need to make happen—in my writing, in my personal life, in my photography—for those things I will turn every stone possible, tirelessly. Even if I don't reach all or even half of my goals and dreams, I'll have the satisfaction of knowing I used every ounce of every skill, talent, and time I had and made it count.

Amazing, razzle-dazzle magic happens and goals shift and evolve, and that's normal and a miraculous part of the process. I'll know I didn't dream of writing books and being a writer. I made it happen with dedication, humor, some frustration, and a bevy of rejection; but I did all I could whenever I could and kept making, making, making good things to put into the world, whether or not the world cared. There is peace of mind and heart in that.

Equally fulfilling: I've gotten to be a small part of the writing and publishing journeys of many of my diverse students of all ages and backgrounds who accomplished the same book-writing dream, so I know it's not only possible but probable.

If there's a book in you (and I believe there is or you wouldn't be checking out this book), write it. Begin and begin and begin.

My gift to you, in the wise words of my family friend: "'If there's anything you want to do, do it. Don't wait.'" You're ready. Write your book.

Acknowledgments

No writer is an island, and it certainly benefits writer and book alike to have the support of thoughtful, steadfast friends, family, and colleagues. My sincere thanks for making this book possible and polished to a shine to the following writers and cohorts, many of them writers and all of them readers extraordinaire:

To my Dream Team at Vine Leaves Press: Jessica Bell for the fabulous encouragement and sublime cover designs; Amie McCracken for superb organization, communication, and answers to my "quick question" emails this year; and Alexis Paige, fellow Gen Xer and rad editor for insights and edits that improved this book's readability by a bunch (a hearty Bravocado to you! #teambravocado). Always a pleasure to work with you.

Many thanks to Antonia Alba, Lee Ann Smith, Kandace "Kandy" Chapple, Mari McCarthy, and Tricia McDonald for invaluable assistance, kind words, camaraderie, and cheering on this book while it was still in its draft phase. Much appreciated!

As always, many thanks to my parents, Thom and Linda Faith, for always believing in me and my writing dreams and for supplying me with endless books and time to read as a child, along with encouraging my imagination every step of the way. Thanks, Mom, for loaning me, when I was still a teenager, the blue typewriter Dad bought you when *you* were teenagers, and for the endless ribbons and bottles of correction fluid through 1,001 drafts. Thanks, Dad, for identifying with the joys of falling down the rabbit hole of a good book and sometimes (okay, often) being reluctant to reemerge for at least another twenty pages.

To my sister, Amanda McGrath, and her family—Adam, Cora Vi, and Sylvie Ro, for being my cheering section through this ongoing writing and teaching life. A special shout-out in this book for my younger niece, Sylvie, who recently asked me for a book series for our birthday, "because you like to buy us books." #truth #myniecesknowmewell May you and your sister long savor books and see them as the gifts they are. You and your sister, Cora, are splendid gifts in my life. Read on!

Thanks to the writers whose books have kept me entertained and edified; your work has been a meaningful part of my training as an author.

For my writing professors and teachers who took their time, talent, energy, and vision to nourish my writing spark long before it was a flame. Thanks so much for the margin comments and your belief in my path. If I can offer my readers and students even half of what you so generously invested in me, then I'll be a grateful educator indeed.

Merci beaucoup to my wonderful students and many literary friends for keeping life lively and inspired amidst trying, unprecedented times. Amidst the topsy-turvy uncertainty, your emails, posts, and writing provided some much-needed continuity. I took these quarantine months (and months) and wrote this book and some others. Your talent and motivation continue to inspire me.

Last but certainly not least: thanks to YOU, dear reader, for spending your precious time with these chapters. It's my deepest hope that this was a good, rejuvenating reading experience for you. May this book encourage and share your writing path as you bring your books into being. Write on!

Vine Leaves Press

Enjoyed this book?
Go to *vineleavespress.com* to find more.